Collins
Webster's

175 YEARS OF DICTIONARY PUBLISHING

easy learning
WRITING

HarperCollins Publishers
Westerhill Road
Bishopbriggs
Glasgow
G64 2QT

First edition 2011

Reprint 10 9 8 7 6 5 4 3 2 1 0

© HarperCollins Publishers 2011

ISBN 978-0-00-736381-0

Collins ® is a registered trademark of
HarperCollins Publishers Limited

www.collinslanguage.com

A catalogue record for this book is
available from the British Library

Typeset by Davidson Publishing
Solutions, Glasgow

Printed in Great Britain by Clays Ltd,
St Ives plc

Editorial staff

American English consultant:
Orin Hargraves

Written by:
Elizabeth Walter
Kate Woodford

Editor: Lisa Sutherland

For the publisher:
Gerry Breslin
Lucy Cooper
Kerry Ferguson
Elaine Higgleton

introduction

Collins Webster's Easy Learning Writing is suitable for anyone who wants to write clear, elegant English, whether at school, at home, or at work. It is written in a simple, clear way, with lots of examples showing how the guidance given can be put into practice.

The book has three main parts:

The first part deals with the things you need to know before you can write effectively. The topics covered here apply to all types of writing, and range from planning your writing to checking it at the end. There are sections on the best way to present your writing on the page, on how to structure longer documents, and on many tricky issues such as how to write speech, abbreviations, numbers, and more. In addition, there is a comprehensive section on style, covering areas such as writing plain English, avoiding ambiguity, and writing with the appropriate level of formality.

The second part of the book takes a detailed look at different types of writing, from informal emails and letters to formal essays, reports, and presentations. It gives advice on structure, tone, and style, and examples of good practice, as well as providing suggestions for useful words and phrases to use in your own work.

The third part covers grammar, punctuation, and spelling. It gives the basic rules that you need to know, draws attention to common mistakes, and shows you how to avoid them.

We hope *Collins Webster's Easy Learning Writing* will help you to write with confidence and success.

Elizabeth Walter & Kate Woodford, 2011

contents

PART ONE
Preparing to write
Thinking about your writing 2
Organizing your ideas 5
Research 9
Making notes and
  summaries 11
Outlines 13
Writing a draft 15

Presentation
General layout 18
Fonts and typefaces 22
Bullets 23
Numbered lists 25
Headers, footers, and
  page numbers 26
Using images 27
Tables and boxes 28
Charts and diagrams 29

Structure
Logical ordering 34
Introductions 35
Conclusions 37
Headings 39
Paragraphs 42

Style
What is good style? 44
Writing in sentences 46
Using plain English 48
Active or passive verbs? 49
Avoiding clichés 50
Avoiding redundancy
  (unnecessary words) 52

Avoiding ambiguity 53
Register 55
Tone 57
Emphasis 60
Avoiding offense 64
Increasing your vocabulary 67
Using a dictionary 69
Terms used in writing
  English 71

Special information
Speech 76
Questions 79
Quotations 81
Proper nouns 86
Abbreviations 88
Numbers 91
Dates 93
Foreign words and phrases 94

Checking your work
General checks 96
Checking spelling 97
Checking grammar and
  punctuation 98
Other things to check 99
Checking work written on
  a computer 100
Marking your corrections 101

PART TWO
Writing
Formal or work emails 104
Letters 121
Blogs 140
Essays 144

contents

Papers, theses, and
   dissertations 157
Reports 162
Presentations 176
Your work qualifications 187
Instructions 191
Leaflets and flyers 198

PART THREE
Grammar
Main verbs 206
Auxiliary verbs 208
Modal verbs 209
Phrasal verbs 210
Nouns 211
Countable and
   uncountable nouns 212
Pronouns 213
Adjectives 217
Adverbs 221
Determiners 224
Prepositions 225
Conjunctions 226
Tenses 227
Subject, object and
   indirect object 232
Agreement 233

Punctuation
The apostrophe 238
The comma 243
Quotation marks 247
Capital letters 249

The period 251
The question mark 253
The exclamation point 254
The colon 255
The semicolon 257
Parentheses 258
Brackets 259
The hyphen 260
Dashes 262
The slash 264

Spelling
Why is spelling
   important? 266
Ways to improve your
   spelling 267
Suffixes and prefixes 268
Forming plurals 271
-ize or -ise? 274
i before e except after c 275
Silent letters 276
Contractions 277

**Common mistakes and
   controversial issues**
Words that are often
   confused 280
Words that are often
   misspelled 291
Common mistakes and
   controversial issues 295

Index 312

Preparing to write

PART ONE

Thinking about your writing

Whatever you are writing, it is important to think about it first.
If you plan your writing well, it will be **clear**, **logical**, **and effective**.

You may think that planning your writing is just one extra job, and a
waste of time, but in fact good planning will probably **save you time**
as well as making your writing better.

Planning does not necessarily take a lot of time, and you do not always
need to make a **written plan**. For instance, it would be silly to make a
written plan for a text message – the whole point is that texting is a
quick way of communicating. However, even with a text message,
you should plan **in your mind**, so that you know what you want to say.

For longer pieces of writing, such as essays, reports, and often even
letters, it is very useful to make a written plan. A plan will help you:

- *organize your thoughts*
- *make sure you are clear about what you want to write*
- *make sure you have all the information you need*
- *make sure you don't leave anything out*

> **Key point to remember**
> Planning will save you time and make your writing more
> effective.

Before you start to write, the most important question to ask
yourself is: **What am I trying to achieve?**

The best way to be clear about this is to ask three questions:

1 **Who** is this writing for?
2 **What** do I want to say?
3 **Why** do I want to say it?

Imagine, for example, that you really like animals, and you need a summer job, so you decide to write to the local zoo. In this case, the answers to the questions above could be:

1 The manager or human relations officer of the zoo.
2 That you want a summer job. That you love animals and worked on a farm last year.
3 Because you want to get a summer job in a zoo.

There are important points to remember about each of these questions:

- **Who?** Make sure that you use a suitable style and tone for your audience. Informal language and jokes are fine for your friends, but a job application needs to be more formal.
- **What?** Make sure that what you say is absolutely clear, and that you have included everything you wanted to include.
- **Why?** Make sure that your writing achieves what you want it to achieve. For instance, if you write a letter of complaint, be clear about what you want to happen: are you writing it because you want an apology, or do you want your money back?

Before starting to write, it can sometimes be helpful to make a **brief summary** of what you are trying to achieve. This can help you to concentrate on the most important points of your writing.

When you have finished your writing, you can go back to your summary and check that what you have written achieves what you wanted it to. A good summary will always answer the questions, who?, what?, and why?

Here are two examples of this kind of summary:

> *A survey of students' opinions of the food in our school cafeteria, to be used as the basis of a campaign for better school meals.*

> *A letter of complaint to the manager of the local theater to say that our recent visit was spoiled by the noise of building work going on in the lobby area, and to ask for our money back.*

Your summary can also help you resist the temptation to add too many details or extra points. Remember that many people are busy – if they do not understand your main points quickly, you may not achieve what you hope to achieve.

Key point to remember
Always be clear about the purpose of your writing.

Organizing your ideas

Whatever you are planning to write, you need to organize your ideas: either on paper, on your computer, or in your head.

There are several good things about this stage of writing:

- You do not need to think too much about grammar and spelling.
- You do not need to write whole sentences: single words, phrases, or even pictures are fine.
- You do not need to put your ideas into any kind of order to begin with – that can come later.
- The act of writing things down can give you new ideas.

It is also a good idea to write down things that you don't know!

Say, for instance, you are writing an essay about the causes of World War I, a subject you have been studying in class. You might write down the things you know about, such as the alliances between different countries, the assassination of Archduke Franz Ferdinand, and conflicts over territory in the Balkans.

Then you can add things you do not know, but think you ought to include in your essay. Examples might be: why were these alliances formed?; who killed Franz Ferdinand and why?; what role did imperialism play in the arguments between countries?

These **questions** will help you to see what **further research** you need to do.

> **Tip for success**
> If you write down your ideas, you will not forget them!

When you have written down all your ideas, you need to put them in some kind of **order**. If you have a very clear idea of what your writing will contain, it may be possible to do this right from the beginning.

One simple way to order your ideas is to list them under different **headings**.

For instance, this writer is planning an article for her student magazine about a vacation job overseas:

Reasons to work overseas	Types of work available	Practical issues
chance to travel see real life earn money make new friends work experience	voluntary v. paid teaching farm work tourist industry	legal: work permits, etc. safety cheapest way to travel there how much will I earn?

It can be useful to be able to **move your ideas around**.

One possibility is to use **Post-it® notes** (small pieces of paper with one sticky edge) and arrange them on a table or a wall.

Imagine you are writing a party invitation. You want to include the date and time of the party, what it's celebrating, that you need a reply to your invitation, that friends and partners are welcome, and that you'd like people to bring drinks.

If you write all those things individually on Post-it® notes, you can make sure you include all the points you want to, and in the best order.

A very flexible way of ordering ideas is to use **mind maps**, or **spider maps**. In these maps, you start with the most important, central idea, and work out from there, using branches leading outwards. The more detailed the idea, the further the branches are from the central point.

This writer is planning to write a leaflet about what we can do to protect the environment:

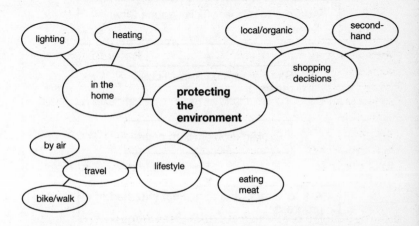

Tip for success
A good mind map will help you structure your writing by showing you how points relate to each other.

Another method that is suitable for some kinds of writing is a **flow chart**. This writer is planning a letter to the local parks authority to ask for repairs to the public basketball court:

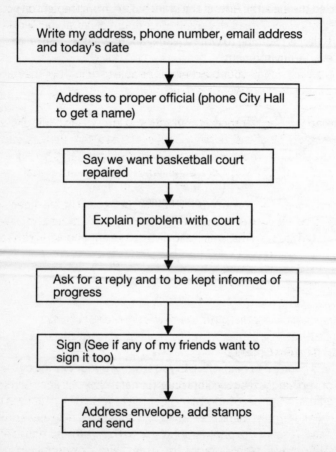

Write my address, phone number, email address and today's date

Address to proper official (phone City Hall to get a name)

Say we want basketball court repaired

Explain problem with court

Ask for a reply and to be kept informed of progress

Sign (See if any of my friends want to sign it too)

Address envelope, add stamps and send

Tip for success

As well as the things you want to write, your flow chart can include things you need to do: for example, finding out a name or address, finding information (e.g., a bank account number), or filling out a form you need to enclose.

Research

For some pieces of writing, especially longer pieces, you will need to do some research. How much you need to do will depend on the information you already have and the amount of detail your writing needs.

If you are a student, your **teacher** will be able to help. They may give you a list of books or websites to use.

Think about whether there is **anybody you know** who could give you information, or at least tell you the best place to look. Perhaps you have a neighbor who works at the local museum, a relative who was alive during World War II, or a friend who is crazy about sports?

A good place to do research is the **library**. Books will be arranged by subject, so it is easy to find what you want. Most libraries also have computerized systems, which allow you to look for books in several ways, for example:

- by subject
- by keywords
  (*important words that give a clue to what the book is about*)
- by author
- by date of publication

It is often useful to ask the **librarians** for help. They will know about all the different sources of information, some of which may not be in book form. For example, many libraries have copies of old newspapers on microfilm (that is, in a photographed form) that you need a special machine to read. Many libraries also have their catalogs online. Looking here first can make your time at the library more efficient if you determine first that the library holds the books you want and you learn where they are located.

Using **the Internet** is a quick and useful way to research a topic. However, it is important to remember that **anyone** can put information on a website. You need to make sure that any source you use is suitable.

A good starting point is to ask two questions:

- **Who** wrote the information you are looking at?
- **What** is the purpose of the site where you found it?

Answering these questions will help you to think about two further questions:

- Is this information likely to be reliable?
- Is the information likely to be fair, or does the writer have a particular purpose, such as supporting an opinion or trying to make you buy something?

Using a **search engine** such as Google®, Yahoo®, or Bing® can be a start, but there is a danger: at first you may find so many sites that you miss the ones that are really important. Many teachers and professors include websites on their reading lists, so if you have been given a reading list, make sure you use it. Otherwise, think about sites that will be reliable. For instance, in the US you might look for medical information on the National Institutes of Health site (http://www.nih.gov). In the UK you could look at the National Health Service site (http://www.nhs.uk).

Tip for success
If you are using the Internet in a library, the librarian may be able to help you find suitable sites.

Making notes and summaries

When you are doing research, you will want to **make notes**. Your notes can be in whatever form suits you best. The important thing is to make sure you will still understand them when you come to use them!

Make sure that the notes you take **relate to the subject** you will be writing about. There is no point adding extra information – however interesting it is – that you will not be able to use.

Notes should be **short** – do not copy out or cut and paste huge pieces of text. In order to **summarize**, it is very important to make sure you have understood the main points. When you have read a chapter or an article, it can be useful to try to write down the most important three or four points in it.

Look for clues in what you are reading to help you:

- Are there any words that are <u>underlined</u> or in **heavy type**?
- Do the headings summarize the main points?
- Does the book itself include summaries or lists of main points?

Use abbreviations, shorten words, or leave out words altogether. "Vikings > N America 900CE" is much more efficient than writing "The Vikings came to North America in 900 CE."

> **Key point to remember**
> Make sure you will be able to understand your notes
> when you need to use them.

If you have a good idea of the structure of your piece of writing, it can be useful to organize your notes.

For example, if you are writing an essay about a book you have read, you may be asked to look at particular things, such as the way the author builds up characters; the style of language used; the way the plot develops; and the author's relationship with the reader.

If you divide your paper into **themes** like these, you can order your notes as you take them. This will make it easier to organize your essay, and also help you balance the amounts of material you have on each theme.

You may use your notes to record good **quotations** to use in your own writing, but be careful:

- If you use a direct quotation, you must reproduce it accurately, and you must say where it has come from.
- If you summarize what someone has said, you must change it into your **own words**. Copying the words of others is called **plagiarizing**. It is not allowed in academic work, and it can be illegal.

Tip for success
While you are making notes, keep a list of **useful words and phrases** to use in your own writing.

Outlines

For longer pieces of writing, it is useful to produce an outline before you start. An outline can have as much or as little in it as you think will be useful for you, but it should at least include a basic list of **headings**. If you have organized your ideas and notes in some of the ways suggested above, you will probably find it fairly easy to produce an outline.

Start by picking out a number of main points – these will be the framework for your writing, and will lead to more detailed points within them.

For some types of writing, such as a report, it may be appropriate to keep these headings in the final text. For others, the headings will simply be a way of organizing your writing and will not appear in your finished work.

You can use your outline to check that everything you want to write is in a **logical order**:

- Make sure that understanding one part does not rely on another part that comes later.
- If you move on to a different point, see if it needs some sort of introduction or explanation.
- Make sure that all the points connected to a particular idea are treated together.

The person who made the following outline is writing a report on the use of volunteers in a local charity:

Volunteer report

Introduction

- what this report covers
- research and methods used
- purpose of report

Summary of main points

The current situation

- number of volunteers
- what they do
- how they are managed

Problems with the current situation

- not enough volunteers
- volunteers not clear about their role
- lack of communication with paid employees

Suggestions for improvement

- better targeting of recruitment campaigns
- written handbook for volunteers
- regular employee/volunteer meetings

Conclusion

> **Key point to remember**
> Use your outline to make sure everything is included and is in the best order.

Writing a draft

A draft is a rough version of your finished writing. It can be as close to or as far away from the final text as you like. For instance, you may decide to concentrate on the content and not worry about spelling and punctuation – that is up to you. If you are writing something very long, or very important, you may write **more than one draft**.

When you have written a draft, it is useful to ask the following questions:

- Does the **order** of what you have written make sense?

- Have you **included everything** you wanted to include?

- Is all the material **relevant**? Is there anything you should cut out?

- Is the **tone** right? For instance, if it is a letter of complaint, is it firm and assertive or is it offensive and rude?

- Does any part need **more explanation**, more information or more evidence?

- Is the amount of **space given to each theme** appropriate, or is one part too long or too short?

- Does it **achieve** what you want it to achieve? (If you wrote a brief summary at the beginning, you can check against it.)

It can sometimes be useful to give a draft of your writing to **someone else**, and ask if what you have written is clear, interesting, and effective – having another person's opinion can be very valuable in giving you a different perspective. That person might make suggestions for additions or improvements, or check facts for you.

Presentation

General layout

A clear and attractive layout will make your writing both more enjoyable to read and easier to understand.

The use of computers makes it easy for everyone to present their writing in a professional way, and gives us lots of choices about how to do this. One of the most useful things about using a computer is that you can edit text and move it around as you work. You can experiment with different ways of presenting it – you do not have to decide on your layout at the beginning.

Here are some general rules:

* Almost all documents look better if there is plenty of **space** around the words.
* Do not make your **sentences or paragraphs** too long.
* Do not make the **size of type** too small.
* Whatever style you choose for the different parts of your document, make sure you **keep to the same style all the way through**.

> **Tip for success**
> Before you finish your document, look at it using the **print preview** option, to see how it will look on the page when it is printed.

Look at the following piece of text:

> To: all Little League members
> Welcome back to baseball practice! Many of you will know that we
> have new uniforms this season. Each player will need a red shirt and
> helmet; these will be available at the first practice. You also need
> the appropriate glove, and cleats, which can be of any type. Please
> remind your parents that there is a $40 fee to cover coaching and
> transportation to games. See you at practice next week,
> From: Matt (team coach)

Now see how a better layout can make the same information much
easier to read:

> To: All Little League members
>
> Welcome back to baseball practice!
>
> **New uniforms**
> Many of you will know that we have new uniforms this season.
> Each player will need:
>
> - red shirt and helmet (available at the first practice)
> - glove appropriate to your position
> - cleats (any type)
>
> **Fees**
> Please remind your parents that there is a $40 fee to cover coaching
> and transportation to games.
>
> See you at practice next week!
>
> Matt (team coach)

Most pieces of text are divided into paragraphs. Each paragraph discusses one point or idea.

The beginning of a new paragraph can be shown in two ways. The first is to **indent** the first sentence, which means starting it further to the right than the rest of the paragraph, like this:

> Additional research has shown a strong link between smoking and heart disease. In a study of more than 1,000 healthy males, it ...

The second way is to **leave a whole line of space** between paragraphs. If you do this, you do not need to indent the first sentence. Separating paragraphs in this way can help to make the structure of your writing clear by showing where each new point or idea starts and ends. Most computer word processing programs will allow you to arrange your paragraphs in either of these styles automatically.

Try not to leave a heading or a single line of a paragraph at the **end of a page**, or to have the last line of a paragraph at the **top of a page**. It is better to have a larger space than usual at the bottom of a page than to have a small part of the paragraph on its own.

You should also try to avoid having a hyphenated word as the last word on a page. To avoid this, try rewriting your sentence, or use one of the "keep" features in your word processing program to keep certain lines together on a page.

> **Key point to remember**
> Using plenty of white space will make your document easier to read.

You will need to decide how you want the **edges** of your text to look.

> You can set your computer like this, so that the ends of the sentences do not fall in a straight line. This style, called "ragged right" or left-justified, can look natural, and the spacing between each word looks better. It usually results in fewer hyphenated words.

> Alternatively, you can set your computer so that the words form a neat, straight line at both of the edges. This style, called justified, can look neater, but you may find that you get large gaps between some words in order to make them fit and you will probably have more hyphenated words.

You will also have to decide whether or not you want your document to use **hyphens** if a long word comes at the end of a line. If the lines in your document are fairly long, and you are not using extremely long words, it is usually best not to use hyphens. However, if you have short lines, you may need to use hyphens to avoid large spaces between words, especially if you are using justified text.

Hyphens must be used at a suitable breaking point in the word. Your computer will do this for you, but if you are writing by hand, you will need to decide where to put hyphens yourself. If you are not confident about this, consult a dictionary: most dictionaries show "syllabification dots" at the points in a word where you are allowed to break it, like this:

bath·y·scaphe   re·pro·duc·tion   un·im·pres·sion·a·ble

> **Tip for success**
> If you do use hyphens, check the line ends when you have finished to make sure there are no word breaks that could cause confusion, such as leg-end, or thin-king.

Fonts and typefaces

A font is the whole set of letters, numbers, and other characters that share the same design. You will be able to choose fonts when you write documents on your computer. They range from standard fonts that you might use for an essay or a letter, to very unusual and dramatic ones that you might use for a party invitation, a poster, or a sign:

> Dear Ms. Hodges
>   I am writing to inquire about the possibility of a job in your company ...

> *Come to our spooky ghost party!*

The **normal font size** for general texts such as essays is 11 or 12 points. You may want to use larger fonts for headings. Sometimes smaller sizes (usually 10 or 11 points) are used for long quotations.

Fonts like this one, which have very small lines at the ends of letters, are called **serif** fonts, while fonts like this one, which have nothing at the ends, are called **sans-serif** fonts. It is best to use a serif font such as Times New Roman for long pieces of text. Headings are often displayed in a sans-serif font such as Arial or Helvetica, even when the main text is in a serif font.

You can also choose different ways of writing words, for example using *italics*, **bold (also called heavy) type**, ***bold italics***, <u>underlining</u>, or SMALL CAPS.

> **Tip for success**
> Avoid writing more than a few words in CAPITAL LETTERS because they are difficult to read.

Bullets

If you want to separate a list of points from the main part of your text, a simple way to do so is to use bullets. Text arranged in this way can be called a bulleted list.

Bullets are often used when the order of the list is not particularly important, e.g.:

> During this exciting week-long course, students will:
>
> - learn how to gather food in the wild
> - spend two nights in a nearby forest
> - learn how to build a shelter from earth and branches

It is not usual to use periods at the end of text that follows bullets, though if the text is more than one sentence, you may feel it looks better.

You can decide whether or not to use capital letters at the beginning of each bullet. In the example above, capital letters were not used because each bulleted item formed a complete sentence following the introductory phrase "students will ..."

> **Key point to remember**
> The most important thing to remember is that when you have decided whether or not to use capital letters and periods, you should do the same for each item.

Bullets can be introduced by any sort of symbol you think is appropriate:

- Probably the most common type is a circle like this.
- A dash is also an acceptable way to format a bulleted list.

▶ You may want to emphasize your points more with a symbol like this.

♪ Or even choose something completely different if it is relevant to your text.

It is important to make sure that the bullet text matches up grammatically with the words you use to introduce it. If you use a phrase such as "You will need the following:", it is simple to follow it by a list of items.

However, you will often find bulleted text introduced by phrases such as:

To write a successful essay, you should:
Students will have the opportunity to:

In cases like this, make sure you read through the introductory phrase and the bullet text together, to make certain they form a correct sentence. Look at the following:

Students will have the opportunity to:

- canoe in the local river
- learn how to cook on a camp fire
- making lots of new friends

The third point does not make a grammatically correct sentence. It should be "make lots of new friends."

Numbered lists

Numbered lists are used in a similar way to bulleted lists. They are often used to show that the order of items is important or where they show a ranking:

The most common girls' names in the US in 2009 were:

1 Isabella
2 Emma
3 Olivia
4 Sophia
5 Ava

You can use numbers or letters to order your points, and in some cases you may even want to do both, in order to go into more detail about a particular point:

Here is the agenda for Monday's meeting:

1 Minutes of the last meeting
2 Sales reports
   a Europe and the Middle East
   b Americas
   c East Asia
3 Next year's training budget
   a in-house training
   b external courses

Tip for success
When you want to indent a list of points, always use a function such as the **tab key** or the bullet or numbers from the **menu bar**. Do not try to indent using the space bar because the spacing will not be even. Your word processing program may have an icon you can click on to adjust the amount of indent of text you have selected.

Headers, footers, and page numbers

Headers and footers are pieces of text that appear at the top or bottom of the pages of your document but are separate from the rest of the writing on that page.

Typical items that might be put in them include:

- document title
- chapter or section titles
- author name
- copyright information
- date
- document reference

Using headers and footers can make your work look more professional. If you have the same header and footer throughout the whole document, you only need to put the text in once and your computer will do the rest automatically.

It is also possible to use different headers and footers for different sections of a document; for example, for each new chapter or section, or on odd and even pages. This can be useful for readers.

Page numbers can also be added automatically, and placed wherever you want them: at the top or bottom of the page; on the right, left, or in the center.

You can also choose the position, size, font, etc., of your headers and footers. For example, you may want a chapter heading at the top of each page to be fairly large, but a copyright note at the bottom to be quite small.

Using images

Using images can be a great way to liven up your text. Reasons for using images may include:

- helping to explain something – sometimes an image can be clearer than words
- decorating a document such as a party invitation
- emphasizing a brand, for example, by using a company logo

A simple way to get images is to use **clip art** that is available in your word processing software, or downloadable from the Internet.

Come to our party!

If you are using images in a more serious document, you should give them captions, and it will often be necessary to number them so that you can refer to them in the text.

Make sure that your images are an appropriate size for your document – it is easy to change the size of an image on your computer.

> **Key point to remember**
> If you use an image, make sure you are legally allowed to do so. Some images are protected by **copyright**, which means you need the owner's permission to use them, and you may have to pay.

Tables and boxes

If you want to present information in rows and columns, it is a good idea to use a table:

Course schedule

	Group 1	**Group 2**
9.00 -9.30 9.30 – 11.00 11.00- 11.30	*Introductions* *Singing workshop* *Break*	*Introductions* *African drumming* *Break*

You can make tables on your computer, and say how many rows and how many columns you need. You can add more rows and columns later if you need to, and you can change their size and position in the table.

You can also use tables to set out information neatly and then make the actual lines of the box disappear afterwards.

If you want to separate off one section of text from the rest, you can put a box or border around it.

> You can also put a shade or a colored tint inside a box to make it stand out, like this.

There are many different types of boxes and borders to choose from in your computer's word processing program. This one, for example, has a shadow effect.

Charts and diagrams

Charts and diagrams can be a good way to present information, particularly numerical information, which can be much easier to understand when shown this way.

Charts and diagrams are particularly good for information that needs to be analyzed, such as information showing **comparisons**, **patterns**, **and trends**.

All charts and diagrams should be numbered and have a heading. Make sure there is plenty of space around them, and that there is always a reference to them in the text:

> As we can see from table 1 ...

> Fig. 3.8 illustrates the increase in ...

There are many different types of chart and diagram. Think about which one best suits the information you want to present.

Graphs

Graphs such as this one are a good way of showing trends in numbers:

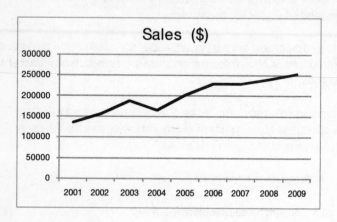

Pie charts

Pie charts are a clear way of showing the relative size of groups of things:

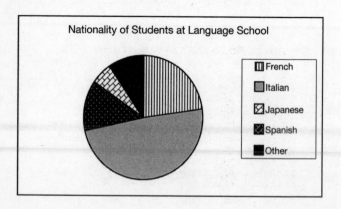

Venn diagrams

Venn diagrams are used to show overlapping groups:

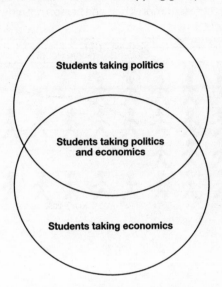

Bar charts

Bar charts also make it easy to compare numbers and amounts:

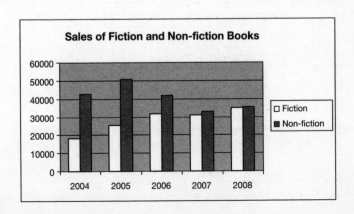

Pictograms

Pictograms are a simple way of showing numbers of people or things. Each image can represent more than one person or thing:

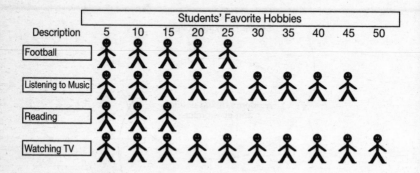

Structure

Logical ordering

If you have planned your writing well, you should have no problem writing it in a logical sequence.

Make sure that your **points lead into each other** in such a way that your reader is guided through your argument. Remember that you should move from general points to more specific, detailed points.

Never include a point without the necessary **background or explanation**, or one that relies on reading something later in the text. Unless you actually refer to other sources, or unless you know that your reader possesses certain knowledge, the text should include all the information needed to understand it.

Make sure that all points of discussion about a particular area of your text come together – **do not change from one topic to another** and then back again.

An essay should **start with an introduction and end with a conclusion**, and in fact there are many types of writing where this is a useful principle, even if it is not done in such a formal way. For instance, if you are writing a formal letter, it can sometimes be helpful to include a short title after the greeting. This acts as an introduction.

Introductions

When you write an essay, you should start with an **introduction** and end with a **conclusion**.

Your introduction will give your readers the information they need to lead them into the main part of the essay.

The introduction should do the following things:

- **Introduce the topic**: briefly describe what the essay is about, providing any necessary explanation of the background and context of the topic.

- **Explain the purpose of the essay**: say what you will discuss, making sure that it fits exactly with the title of your essay. If you have been given a title, be careful to look for words like "examine," "contrast," "describe," or "analyze," and make sure that this is what your essay does.

- **Define your terms**: if there is any possibility of doubt, say exactly what you mean by words and phrases, both in the title and throughout the essay. For instance, if your essay is about childhood diabetes, you should say what age range you consider to be covered by the term *childhood*.

In the same way, if there is any possible doubt about the meaning of the title, you should say very clearly what you understand by it, and how this understanding will form the basis of what follows.

- **Explain how your points are organized**: give a brief summary of the structure of your essay.

An introduction can be more than one paragraph, if necessary. As a general rule, it should be around 10% of the total length of your essay. Remember though, it should not be a summary of the whole thing – if it is, the reader will not bother reading to the end!

Other points you may want to cover in your introduction include:

- **A statement of why your topic is particularly interesting or important.**

- **An explanation of how your work fits into a wider context**: for example, how it relates to research being done by others, or how it is affected by current events or attitudes.

- **A discussion of areas of your topic where there is a lack of knowledge.**

> **Tip for success**
> While a short quotation can be an interesting way to start an essay, avoid long quotations or detailed examples in your introduction.

Conclusions

The introduction and conclusion form a frame for your essay. The conclusion brings together all the ideas and information you have discussed. It shows the reader that the essay is complete and that the aims of the essay have been achieved.

When you write your conclusion, always look back at the introduction. Make sure that your conclusion shows your essay has really done what you said it would do.

A conclusion does two main things:

- **Summarizes** the main points and ideas.

- **Reaches conclusions** by saying what the consequences of your writing are.

By summarizing the main points, you provide your reader with a brief, clear statement of the most important points you have discussed. You should also include a brief reminder of the purpose of this discussion.

Everything that you summarize must be fully covered in the main part of the essay – you should not add any new information here.

As well as summarizing *what* you have discussed, you should summarize what you have said your evidence suggests.

> **Key point to remember**
> Never add any new points or ideas in your conclusion.

The type of conclusions you reach will depend on the question you were dealing with in the essay. You might:

- **Achieve a task set in the title**: For instance, if you were asked to contrast the characters of the Bennet sisters in the novel *Pride and Prejudice*, you would simply summarize the main differences you found.

- **Give your opinion**: For instance, if you were asked to say whether or not nuclear power is a good form of fuel, you would express your opinion and explain briefly how the evidence you have presented supports it.

- **Show what you have learned from looking at evidence**: For instance, if you are asked to analyze the results of a research project on the effects of diet on rates of heart disease, you would summarize the main facts you have discovered from the survey.

- **Make recommendations**: For instance, if you are writing a report on the best way to encourage recycling, you would suggest actions that could be taken.

Often you will find that issues you discuss in essays are complicated and you cannot find a simple answer or give a definite opinion. This is fine – you should simply explain why this is the case by summarizing the main points.

Headings

Headings are often used in long documents. They can **make the presentation more effective and attractive** by breaking up long pieces of text.

Headings are **useful for your readers**. They reveal the structure of your document and enable the reader to find a particular topic easily.

It is best to **start with headings and then write your text**. If you do it like this, your essay will be better organized than if you simply write it and try to add headings afterwards. If you have written an outline, you can often use the points in your outline as headings, modifying them as you work if necessary.

You can use **different levels of heading**. The lower levels are called subheadings. In a long document, main headings mark the major sections and subheadings then divide these sections.

Try not to use too many headings. As a general rule, 2 or 3 headings per letter-size page would be enough. Sometimes you cannot avoid having a very short section under a heading – there may simply be very little to say about that particular point. That is fine, but try not to break up the text too much.

> **Key point to remember**
> Start with your headings, then write your text.

If you are using subheadings, it is even more important to plan your heading structure before you write, so that you have a consistent framework for the whole document. Sections of similar importance should have the same level of heading.

It is usually a good idea to number headings, especially if you want to make a table of contents. It is up to you how you number them, but a common way would be to use a system of numbers and points:

    1.   Main heading
        1.1 subheading
            1.1.1 sub-subheading

Once you have decided on a structure, you need to choose a style for your headings. Make sure the style is the same throughout the whole document.

You will need to think about the following:

- the **font type and font size** for each level of heading
- are your headings **numbered**, and if so how?
- are your headings **bold**, *italic*, <u>underlined</u>, etc.?
- do they start with a **capital letter**?
- do they include **punctuation**?
- how much **space** is there before and after the surrounding text?

> **Tip for success**
> Computer programs like Word® have built-in headings that you can use. You can change the style if you want, then you can simply choose the heading type when you need it.

Try to make your headings as specific as possible. Instead of the heading "Background," for example, try to express what sort of background information you are giving in this section. Make sure that your headings accurately describe the information they include.

Try to think about your headings from the point of view of the reader and the purpose of your document.

For instance, if you are writing an explanation of how to do something, headings with verbs can be effective, e.g.:

- **Planning your vegetable garden**
- **Deciding what to grow**
- **Preparing your soil**

Sometimes it is appropriate to use questions as headings, e.g.:

- **What is a carbon footprint?**
- **How can I reduce my carbon footprint?**

The reader should be able to read separately from the headings. Do not use pronouns in the first sentence that refer back to the heading. For example, if your heading is "Principles of the carbon cycle" do not begin the next sentence "This is the process ...."

> **Tip for success**
> Before you print your document, check to make sure that there are no headings on their own at the bottom of pages.

Paragraphs

In a long piece of writing, such as an essay or a report, each paragraph should contain one separate point or idea.

The **first sentence** of each paragraph usually introduces what the paragraph is about:

- *Smith's views have, however, been challenged by several experts.*
  (Continue by explaining what the experts say.)

- *This new law gave greater protection to workers.*
  (Continue by describing how it did so.)

Here are some useful phrases to link your paragraphs:

- **As a result of** *this research, scientists have decided ...*
- **Meanwhile**, *my brothers had been busy ...*
- **Despite** *these problems, they carried on trying to ...*
- **Nevertheless**, *she was forced to ...*
- **However**, *we did not allow ourselves to ...*
- **On the other hand**, *many people say that ...*
- **In addition to** *this work on dolphins, he ...*

> **Tip for success**
> Try not to make your paragraphs too long. If they are
> very long, you will probably find that they can be divided
> into separate points.

Style

What is good style?

When people write with good style, their writing is clear, interesting, elegant and appropriate for their audience.

The best style to use will vary according to the type of document you are writing: the kind of original, descriptive writing you would use for a piece of creative writing would not be appropriate for a factual report.

There are many aspects to writing with good style, which are discussed in this section.

However, one simple rule applies to all your work:

Avoid repeating words.

Whatever you are writing, it will sound dull and clumsy if you use the same words over and over again. If you read your work aloud, you will notice when you have done this.

Too much repetition	Better ...
Team A discovered ..., Team B discovered ..., Team C discovered ...	*Team A discovered ..., Team B found ..., Team C's results showed ...*

Sometimes the easiest way to avoid repetition is simply to replace one of the words with a pronoun:

Too much repetition	Better ...
We intend to invite all our friends and ask each friend to bring some food.	*We intend to invite all our friends and ask each of them to bring some food.*

However: just as you avoid repetition, you should avoid the habit called "elegant variation," which is using a difficult and unfamiliar synonym just because you don't want to use a simpler word again. The best way to avoid elegant variation is to avoid using a word that is not familiar to you – perhaps one that you have found in a list of synonyms in a thesaurus. Such a word will probably stand out awkwardly in your text and will not do the job you want it to do.

Writing in sentences

Sentences are the building blocks of texts. The length of your sentences will depend on who you are writing for. Very long sentences can be confusing, while very short sentences can sound childish and can be irritating to the reader. If your sentence is longer than about 15–20 words, see if you can divide it.

The basic rule is that each sentence should have **a subject and a predicate**:

> *The vase smashed on the floor.*
> (vase = subject, smashed on the floor = predicate)
> *My Mom plays the violin.*
> (My Mom = subject, plays the violin = predicate)

Note that the predicate of a sentence always contains a verb.

Some people think it is bad style to end a sentence with a preposition such as *on*, *up* or *in*. However, avoiding this can sometimes lead to a rather formal style. Compare the following:

> *We were shocked to see the conditions they live in.*
> *We were shocked to see the conditions in which they live.*

As always, think about the reader and the purpose of your document to help you choose the appropriate style and tone.

> **Tip for success**
> Try reading your work aloud; if your sentences work well, it will be easy to read. See where you make natural pauses, and think about whether you need to add commas, semicolons, or other punctuation.

Do not string lots of sentence parts together using commas. This is a common mistake, and can be confusing.

Look at the following:

> *First we went to the Statue of Liberty, which was fantastic, our tour guide was excellent, and we saw Ellis Island, later we had our picnic on the lawn outside the museum.*

This sentence would be much better using dashes and splitting it into separate sentences, like this:

> *First we went to the Statue of Liberty, which was fantastic – our tour guide was excellent. After that we saw Ellis Island, and later we had a picnic on the lawn outside the museum.*

However, make sure you use commas where they are needed, as they can help the reader understand your sentences better.

For instance, commas are needed if a subordinate clause (less important part of a sentence) comes before the main clause, e.g.:

> *If the flight is late, call before you take off.*

They are also needed for adding small pieces of information about someone or something in your sentence, e.g.:

> *My sister, who is a vet, has three children.*

Tip for success
Take care with punctuation. There is a detailed explanation of how to use commas and other punctuation marks in the punctuation section of this book.

Using plain English

It is important to write in plain English. Plain English is easier to write, and certainly easier to understand. Try to follow these rules:

- **Avoid unnecessary jargon.** Don't talk about "interfacing" with someone when you mean "communicating" with them, or simply "talking" to them. Don't say "design solution" – it's just a design.

Of course, there are times when technical and specialist terms *are* appropriate. If your audience consists only of people who work in a particular field, they will expect you to use the terms they are familiar with. And if you are writing a scientific or technical essay, you must use the correct terminology. As always, think of your reader.

- **Avoid unnecessary formality.** Ask yourself if there is a simpler word or phrase that would be appropriate for your reader.

very formal	simpler ...
prior to	before
in excess of	more than
in the vicinity of	near

- **Try to use active verbs instead of nouns.** This will make your sentences sound less complex and formal.

noun form	active verb form
give encouragement to	encourage
ensure the completion of	complete
make provision for	provide
make utilization of	use

Active or passive verbs?

It is usually better to use active verbs in your writing because the structure is simpler. Passive verbs can sometimes sound formal. Compare these two sentences, for example:

> *New recycling methods have been introduced by the county.* (Passive.)
> *The county has introduced new recycling methods.* (Active.)

However, the passive can be useful in certain cases. For instance, you may use the passive if you do not want to appear to be blaming someone or criticizing someone:

> *You have not paid the fine.* (Active and accusing.)
> *The fine has not been paid.* (Passive and more neutral.)

You may also want to use the passive if you do not want your reader to blame you:

> *I'm sorry to report that I have lost your documents.* (Active and admitting fault.)
> *I'm sorry to report that your documents have been lost.* (Passive and implying that it may have been someone else's fault.)

The passive is also used when you do not know who carried out an action or it is irrelevant who carried out the action. This will often happen in academic writing in which the slightly more formal style is appropriate:

> *The results were analyzed in the laboratory.*
> *The buildings were knocked down in 1989.*

Avoiding clichés

A cliché is a word or phrase that has been used too often. If you use clichés, your writing may be boring or irritating. When readers find too many clichés, they may lose interest and miss your main message. They may think that if your writing is not original, your ideas cannot be original either.

You may find that clichés slip into the first draft of your writing – after all, it is because they are so well known and come so easily to mind that they have become clichés. Read through your document and try to identify any phrases that seem to fit into this category. If English is not your first language, it may be difficult to do this. In this case, it may be a good idea to ask a native English speaker for advice.

Then ask yourself: what does this phrase actually mean? It may not really have much meaning at all, in which case you can probably delete it. Examples of this sort of cliché are:

> *when all is said and done*
> *at this point in time*
> *with all due respect*
> *in any way, shape, or form*
> *going forward*

Or it may be that the phrase has been used so much that it has lost all its power, and may well annoy your reader. Examples of this sort of cliché are:

> *move the goalposts*
> *reinvent the wheel*
> *the best thing since sliced bread*

Sometimes a simple **combination of adjective and noun** can be so overused that it becomes a cliché, e.g.:

> *roaring fire*
> *vise-like grip*
> *long-lost friend*

This does not mean that such combinations should never be used, but try not to use too many obvious combinations, and choose something more original if you can.

One area of language where it is very easy to fall into the trap of using a cliché is the **simile**.

Look at the following similes:

> *as cold as ice*
> *as fresh as a daisy*

They are so overused that they are not powerful descriptions.
Now look at the following similes, all found in real writing:

> *as cold as a Siberian winter*
> *as cold as a stone statue*
> *as fresh as green shoots in the morning*

Of course, imaginative similes like these are not suitable for all types of writing. In formal writing, it may be best to avoid similes altogether. In more creative writing, you should aim to be descriptive and original, but your similes should fit into the overall style of the text.

Avoiding redundancy (unnecessary words)

It is very easy to use more words than you need, and too many words will make your writing less effective and may annoy your readers.

Compare the following:

> *Jack and I are of the same opinion on this matter.*
> *Jack and I agree.*

> *Due to the fact that the train was delayed, we were late for the concert.*
> *We were late for the concert because the train was delayed.*

Avoid "empty" words and phrases that do not add meaning to your sentences, e.g., *in terms of, the fact of the matter*.

Avoid saying the same things twice. This is known as **tautology**. Consider the following:

9 a.m. in the morning	a.m. means "in the morning" – choose one or the other
reexamine again	just say "reexamine" – the "again" is expressed in the prefix "re-"
my personal opinion	if it's your opinion, it's personal – you don't need to say so
mutual cooperation	you can't cooperate on your own, so it must be mutual

Avoid adding illogical extra words. Consider the following:

in actual fact	if it is a fact, it must be "actual" – just say "in fact"
very unique	something unique is the *only* one of its kind – there are no degrees of uniqueness

Avoiding ambiguity

Ambiguity is when something could possibly be understood in more than one way. It is an easy trap to fall into because *you* know what you mean when you write, but try to put yourself in the reader's place and make sure there is no room for doubt.

Be careful with **words that have more than one meaning**. Often the context will be enough to make it clear which meaning is intended. If you write that you are going to the bank, nobody is likely to think you are going to a river bank. However, consider the following:

> *My teacher is really funny.*
> (Is the teacher humorous or strange?)

> *The food was very hot.*
> (Was it a high temperature, or was it spicy?)

Make it clear whether you are using words and phrases in a **literal or figurative** sense:

> *He was in debt to his friend.*
> (Did he owe his friend money or simply feel grateful?)

> *There was a chasm between us.*
> (Was there a hole in the ground, or a big difference of opinion?)

Use pronouns carefully to make sure it is clear who or what they refer to:

> *Rosie had an argument with Sarah, and she started crying.*
> (Who cried, Rosie or Sarah?)

> *I couldn't attach the bird boxes to the posts in the field because they weren't strong enough.*
> (Was it the posts or the bird boxes that weren't strong?)

Check the structure of your sentence to make sure it is clear how the parts relate to each other. Compare the following:

> *We talked about bullying at work.*
> (Ambiguous – were we at work or not?)

> *We talked about the issue of workplace bullying.*
> *At work, we talked about bullying.*

> *They told us about the murder at 11 o'clock.*
> (Ambiguous – did the murder happen at 11 o'clock?)

> *At 11 o'clock, they told us about the murder.*
> *They told us about the murder that occurred at 11 o'clock.*

Make sure it is clear what your adjectives are describing:

> *a large woman's handbag*
> (Is it the woman or the handbag that is large?)

> *a formal English test*
> (Is the test formal, or is it a test of formal English?)

Be clear about the purpose of your writing. Imagine that you receive a memo that includes the following:

> *It would be a good idea for all employees to take at least 30 minutes for lunch.*

It would not be clear whether the memo is saying that you *must* take 30 minutes or simply that it would be a nice thing if possible.

Register

The word 'register' refers to aspects of language such as how formal or informal it is. Compare the following:

> *They furnished us with the requisite implements.* (Very formal.)
> *They gave us the necessary tools.* (Neutral.)
> *They let us have the gear we needed.* (Informal.)

You should match the register of your language to the type of writing you are doing. Using the wrong register can make your writing sound odd and can even cause offense.

Register can often be shown by the choice of words or phrases:

formal or literary	neutral	informal
wax lyrical	speak enthusiastically	rattle on
precisely	exactly	on the nose
in ascendancy	becoming successful	climbing up

Dictionaries mark words that are formal or informal, so you can check if you are not sure. Many idioms and phrasal verbs are either informal or slightly informal, so take care to use them appropriately.

Informal language is fine for personal letters, emails, texts, etc., but for most forms of writing, a neutral style is more appropriate. You may want to use a slightly formal style when writing for an audience older than you or for an audience that you have some obligation to. Remember, though, that formal does not mean pompous. Do not use very formal language to try to impress – it is more important to put your ideas across clearly.

> **Tip for success**
> Do not use different registers within the same piece of writing.

Sometimes words and phrases with a particular register are needed for specific types of writing. For instance, **legal documents** often contain extremely formal language, such as *hereunder* or Latin words such as *ex gratia*, which would be out of place in most other types of writing.

Similarly, some types of writing need to use very specific **technical terms**. For example, a document for medical professionals might use a word such as *suprarenal* instead of saying "above the kidneys" because this word will be understood by its readers. In scientific documents, the use of technical terms can be necessary to avoid any ambiguity.

At the other end of the scale, **literary or poetic language** such as *lovelorn*, *flaxen* or *the gloaming* may be appropriate in some types of creative writing.

Your choice of **grammar** and the way you **structure** your sentences can also affect register. Compare the following:

> *The man to whom I gave my ticket.*
> *The man I gave my ticket to.*

In the first sentence, the use of *whom* gives a formal feel to the sentence. In the second sentence, the preposition is used at the end. In the past this was considered incorrect, but it is now widely accepted, and would be appropriate for most types of writing.

It is not usually considered appropriate to use contractions (e.g., don't, he'd, wouldn't) in formal writing because they make the text sound informal.

Tone

The tone of your writing expresses your **attitude** towards the reader, and it is important that you be careful about this.

For instance, if you are writing to complain about a product or service, you need to come across as being assertive and clear about your facts. You must decide for yourself whether you want to be rude or threatening too – but if you are, make sure it is on purpose and not because you have chosen your words badly!

It can be useful to **imagine that you are talking to your reader**. What sort of tone do you want to take? For example, you might be:

chatty	authoritative	sincere	sympathetic
grateful	serious	assertive	humorous
persuasive	practical	unfriendly	offended
efficient	angry		

If you **think about what you want to achieve** with your writing, it will help you decide what tone to take. For example, if you are writing a letter to accept a job, you will probably want your tone to be friendly yet professional and show that you are pleased to have been chosen.

It is important to use language that is the **right level of difficulty** for your reader. If you use difficult words, you may sound as if you are showing off, but if you use very simple language, your reader might feel you are talking down to them.

An important issue that influences tone is the **relationship of the writer to the reader**. For instance, a suggestion for changes to working practices might have a very different tone coming from a junior employee than if it comes from a senior manager.

You should always take into account **how well you know the person** who will read your document. If you do not know them at all, you must be aware that they may be offended by an informal tone that is too familiar, or by expressing views that they may not share. Humor can also be difficult – if your readers do not know you, they may be unsure whether you are joking or not.

Compare the following letters:

> Dear Emma
>   Tom told me you broke your leg skiing – after I'd stopped laughing, it occurred to me that you must be a bit out of it, so I'm sending you these chocolates to cheer you up. See you when (if???) you can walk again,
> Lizzie, x

> Dear Emma
>   I'm so sorry to hear about your skiing accident. Your mother told me you are likely to be in a cast for weeks, and I know how hard that will be for you. Do take good care of yourself, and I hope to hear some better news of you soon,
> with love from
> Aunt Bea

In the first letter, the tone is chatty and humorous, and while it might make Emma smile, if her injury is serious she might be offended that her friend is joking about it. However, if Lizzie is a very close friend, she will probably have judged the tone of the note appropriately. The second letter is much more sincere and serious and the tone shows that the writer is really concerned about Emma.

If you are angry about something, it can be very easy to let it show, sometimes without intending to. For example, look at this email:

> *Thanks for your offer of database training, but I really don't feel it's necessary, and I wouldn't want to distract you from your work, which is already behind schedule.*

The tone of the email makes it clear that the writer was offended by the offer of help and takes revenge by implying that the person offering help cannot manage their own work.

This may be what the writer intends, but if you would prefer to keep a good relationship with your colleague, something like the following would be better:

> *Thanks for the offer of database training, but I think I've managed to get to grips with it now, and I wouldn't want to take up your time unnecessarily as I know you are very busy.*

You should always think twice about expressing anger or other negative emotions in your writing: things you say aloud may be forgotten, but once you have written something you have created a record that may live far beyond anyone's memory of it.

Key point to remember
The tone you choose is up to you, but if your writing expresses an attitude, make sure this is what you intend.

Emphasis

We use emphasis to draw a reader's attention to the points that are most important. There are several ways of doing this:

- **Order within the document**. It is usual to start with the most important points.

- **Order within a sentence or paragraph**. The first part of the sentence will usually be seen as the most important. Compare the following:

  A thorough safety assessment is needed urgently, following a number of accidents on the site.
  Following a number of accidents on the site, a thorough safety assessment is needed urgently.

In the first example, the fact that the safety assessment is needed is emphasized by coming first in the sentence. In the second example, the fact that there have been some accidents comes across as the more important point. If you want to give special emphasis to a subject, consider writing your sentence in a way that isolates the most important thing at the end. For example:

  Following a number of accidents on the site it became clear that one thing was urgently needed: a thorough safety assessment.

- **A summary of main points**. This can be done in the conclusion of a document, or even as a list. For example, a detailed report might start with a section on "key findings" or "key recommendations" – simply a list of the main points the author wishes to make.

- **Amount of text**. The more important a point, the more space you are likely to use discussing it. If you add too much detail about minor points, readers may be confused about what is most important.

- **Blank space around a key phrase or sentence.** This is a somewhat dramatic way of emphasizing a key point but it may be appropriate in some kinds of writing:

  The evidence led to one clear conclusion:
  He did not kill his wife.

- **Typeface**. It is very simple to highlight words and phrases by using different forms of typeface such as **bold**, *italics* or <u>underlining</u>. Italics are probably the most commonly used:

  Students should not bring cell phones to class *at any time*.
  Make sure you take *all* your belongings with you.

Fonts can also be made larger or smaller for emphasis, or a different color may be used to make certain parts of a document stand out. Do not use color for emphasis, however, unless you are sure that your document will always be reproduced in color.

- **Repetition**. Repetition can be used in several ways to emphasize points. You could make a point and then repeat it immediately, using phrases such as:

  In other words …
  Put more simply …

This is a useful way to stress the point you are making and also to explain it in a different way so that you can be certain that all your readers will understand it.

If you are writing a long document, you may want to repeat certain points throughout it, using phrases such as:

  This demonstrates yet again …
  Again we see …

Repetition can also be a useful stylistic advice, in writing as well as in speech. You might repeat a word, a phrase, or part of a phrase:

> *They said local businesses would close – not true. They claimed jobs would be lost – not true. They claimed traffic would increase – not true.*

- **Headings**. Headings can be used to reinforce the main point that will be made in the parts they refer to.

- **Sudden change of style**. If readers are surprised by a sudden change of style, they may pay more attention to what is being said. One example would be to use a very short, snappy sentence after one or more longer, more flowing sentences:

> *Architects and engineers had assured officials and residents that the techniques used in constructing the bridge would ensure that it remained solid during an earthquake. It did not.*

- **Emphatic words and phrases**. These can highlight the most important points, e.g.:

> *Our priority now is ...*
> *The crucial advantage that this plan offers is ...*

In a similar way, sentence adverbs such as *crucially* or *above all* signal the importance of what follows, as do adjectives such as *urgent*, *vital*, or *essential*.

- **Punctuation.** The most obvious way to emphasize a sentence is to end it with an exclamation point:

> *We won over a thousand dollars!*

Be careful with exclamation points, though. It is fine to use them in informal letters, emails, etc., but do not use them too often. It is not usually appropriate to use them in more formal writing.

Structuring a sentence with a dash or a colon can also emphasize part of it. See, for example, how the second of these two sentences has more emphasis:

> *Critics described his performance as terrible.*
> *Critics had one word for his performance: terrible.*

Avoiding offense

A simple rule for avoiding offense is this:

Treat everyone equally in your writing, regardless of age, sex, race, sexual orientation or physical difference.

Always make sure that you are **aware of the customs and values of your readers**. For instance, for some readers it may be insensitive to assume that couples, even married couples, consist of a man and a woman. Another audience might be offended by the idea that a couple consists of anything except a man and a woman; so it is not always easy to find the correct balance.

Check that the terms you use for sensitive issues such as race and disability are the **modern**, **accepted terms**, and not old-fashioned terms that might be considered offensive.

Race and religion

It goes without saying that offensive racial or religious insults or stereotypes should never be used.

However, it can sometimes be easy to display discrimination without meaning to, simply because of our cultural background. Make sure you follow these general rules:

- **Only mention race or religion if it is relevant to your writing.**
  If you mention someone's race or religion, ask yourself if you would have mentioned it if it was the same as yours.

- **Make sure you use accepted modern terms,** not old-fashioned ones that many now consider offensive. For instance, a term such as *Red Indian* belongs only in old Westerns – for writing today, use *American Indian* or *Native American*. Similarly, the term *African American* is the preferred description for Americans of African origin.

- **Be aware of different cultures.** For instance, don't assume that everyone celebrates Christmas, or that July and August are always the hottest months of the year.

The accepted current term for people whose parent or ancestors are from different races is *mixed-race*. If you are in doubt about any terms connected with race or religion, check a good, recent dictionary.

Sexism

Here are some rules for avoiding sexism in your writing:

- **Use job titles that refer to both men and women**. For example, use *police officer* rather than *policeman*; *chair* or *chairperson* instead of *chairman*; *letter carrier* rather than *mailman*.

- **Avoid the suffix –ess on jobs.** Words like *authoress* and *poetess* are old-fashioned and patronizing, and should not be used. It is best to avoid the *–ess* suffix for jobs altogether: while the words *actress* and *waitress* are still used, many women in these professions prefer *actor* and *server*. Today there are preferred alternatives for most such words, such as *flight attendant* instead of *stewardess*.

- **Do not mention a person's sex if it is not relevant.** It is usually best to avoid terms such as *male nurse* or *lady doctor*.

- **Do not make assumptions about the sex of people in a particular profession.** Do not write things like "*businessmen and their wives*."

- **Avoid stereotypes of roles and characteristics.** It's not necessarily Mom who cooks the dinner and Dad who fixes the car.

- **Avoid using masculine pronouns.** Sentences such as "Each traveler must present his documents" sound old-fashioned and sexist. Most people now consider it acceptable to use the pronoun *their* in such cases.

- **If you write to someone whose sex you do not know, do not begin your letter** *Dear Sir/s*. You could use *Dear Sir/Madam* in very formal situations, or choose another form of address altogether, e.g., *Dear Friends/Dear Supporters*.

Disability

When writing about illness and disability, there are several points to bear in mind:

- **Be sure to use current, accepted terms.** Use *bipolar disorder* rather than *manic depression*, for example.

- **Do not describe someone only by their illness.** Remember that they are a person first of all, so say *someone with epilepsy* rather than *an epileptic*.

- **Try not to portray someone with a disability as a victim.** Avoid words like *victim*, *afflicted with*, *suffering from*. Say *using a wheelchair* rather than *wheelchair-bound*.

- **Do not refer to people without a disability as** *normal*. Say *not handicapped* or *able-bodied* instead.

Increasing your vocabulary

The best way to increase your vocabulary is to **read a lot**. Be sure that your reading includes material that requires you to think and that contains some words that you will have to use a dictionary to understand better.

If you find a word you do not know, you will sometimes be able to get a good idea of its meaning from the other words around it. If not, **look it up in a dictionary**. It is not always a good idea to look up every new word as you find it, because it can be distracting, but you could **underline or highlight** some of the words and look them up later.

It can be useful to **keep a vocabulary notebook**, to record new words you have learned. You can arrange the words in whatever way is best for you: by alphabetical order or by subject.

Try to develop an interest in words, and ask yourself questions about them. For instance, you can widen your vocabulary by learning **words in groups**. If you know that *canine* refers to dogs, see if you know a word of the same kind that relates to cats (*feline*) or to cows (*bovine*). Similarly, if you know that *carnivorous* means "meat-eating," do you know the word for "plant-eating" (*herbivorous*) or for creatures that eat anything (*omnivorous*)?

Notice the context that words are in. You can often make your writing more elegant by choosing which words go together, such as the interesting verbs with the common nouns in these examples:

> **abandon** *an attempt*
> **draw** *to a close*
> **adopt** *a method*

Word games such as **crossword puzzles** can help to develop an interest in words and can introduce words you did not know before.

Using a thesaurus

A thesaurus is a reference book that shows lists of words with similar meanings. Some word processing systems have a thesaurus built into them, so that you can click on a word for suggestions of different words with similar meanings, and there are also many thesauruses online. Look at very common words in your writing and see if there are any more interesting or specific words you could use instead. You can use a thesaurus for this, but be careful to avoid the use of words completely unknown to you; you might well use them incorrectly:

if you have written ...	consider whether you could use ...
difficult	ambitious, demanding, grueling, knotty, laborious
eat	bolt, consume, gulp, sample, wolf down
boring	bland, characterless, dreary, insipid, soul-destroying

Using a dictionary

A good dictionary will help a lot with your writing. Try to use a dictionary that is **suitable for you**. For instance, if you are in school, a special **dictionary aimed at your level of study** should have all the words you need for all your subjects, but not be too big to carry around. If English is not your first language, try to use a **learner's** dictionary, which will have simple definitions, lots of example sentences, and all the grammar information you need.

Digital dictionaries

There are many types of digital dictionary available now. Tiny **handheld** ones are easy to carry around, and may be useful for spelling or quick look-ups, but the screens may be too small to show lots of useful information.

A lot of book dictionaries come with either a **CD-ROM** or with a code that gives you access to an **Internet dictionary**. You can use these easily while you are working on the computer. Some of them will even look up words for you if you put the cursor over the word you want.

CD-ROM and Internet dictionaries can be extremely useful because they can do things that are impossible in paper books. For instance, if you don't know how to spell a word, you can just type in the letters you are sure of, and all the words containing those letters will be found. Many of these dictionaries have extra information such as synonyms and antonyms, the ability to search for vocabulary in topics, and extra examples. You can also hear spoken pronunciations, rather than trying to work them out from symbols.

Information in dictionaries

Dictionaries are not just for meanings and spelling, although of course these are very important uses. Dictionaries can give you information on:

- **Irregular inflections**. If words do not have regular patterns, this will be shown. For instance, you can see that the plural of *genus* is *genera* or that the past participle of *sink* is *sunk*.

- **Variant spellings**. You can see which words have more than one spelling, e.g., *caftan* and *kaftan*.

- **Regional information**. You can see when words and spellings are used in a particular variety of English, e.g., *courgette* is used in British English, but Americans say *zucchini* for the same vegetable.

- **Example sentences**. Many dictionaries give example sentences, showing how to use a word in context.

- **Etymology**. Large dictionaries often give information about the origins of words and phrases. This can be a very useful tool for helping you to remember which words are related to each other through a common ancestor.

- **Register**. A dictionary will tell you if a word is formal, informal, etc.

- **Pronunciation**. This is usually shown using a set of symbols that indicate sounds and stress.

- **Syllabification**. American dictionaries usually show the places in a word that divide syllables; this can be useful if you are writing by hand and need to know where a word can break.

Terms used in writing English

The following are important terms that refer to different styles of writing and types of words and phrases. You need to know them for studying literature, and also to be aware of them for use in your own writing.

Antonym

An antonym is a word with an opposite meaning. *Legal* and *illegal* are antonyms, as are *mature* and *immature*.

Alliteration

Alliteration is the use of the same letter or sound (especially consonants) at the beginning of two or more words that are close together in a sentence:

> *droplets of dew at dawn*

Assonance

Assonance is the repetition of vowel sounds in two or more words that are close together in a sentence:

> *I laughed, but my heart was torn apart.*

Euphemism

A euphemism is a word or phrase that is used to avoid talking directly about something that is embarrassing, upsetting, or offensive.

Euphemisms can be used in personal writing to show tact to your reader. For instance, in a letter of sympathy, some people prefer to use the euphemism *passed away* rather than *died*. Euphemisms can be used to avoid embarrassment to readers who are uncomfortable with words connected with sex or bodily functions.

Euphemisms are sometimes used in formal writing to deliberately disguise an unpleasant truth. For instance, a company press release might talk about *restructuring* or *downsizing* rather than *laying off employees*. In war, the terms *collateral damage* or *friendly fire* sound much less terrible than the reality of what they describe.

There is no place for euphemism in scientific or technical writing.

Figurative language

Figurative language is where an extra, more imaginative meaning comes from a literal meaning. For instance, the literal meaning of the word *chasm* is "a large hole in the ground," whereas the figurative meaning refers to a fundamental difference of opinion between people.

Idioms

Idioms are phrases such as *give someone a hand* and *be over the moon*, where the meaning is not the same as the literal meaning of all the words in the phrase.

Metaphor

Metaphor is the use of a particular word or phrase – usually a concrete noun – to describe the characteristics of something else. For instance, we might say *She has a heart of ice*, meaning that she shows no sympathy or emotion.

Proverbs

Proverbs are short sentences that many people know, often expressing advice, or something that many people believe to be true. Examples of proverbs are *A stitch in time saves nine* and *Spare the rod and spoil the child*.

Similes

Similes are phrases such as *as red as a beet* or *sing like an angel*, which compare one thing to another. The difference between a simile and a metaphor is that similes say that something is *like* something else, whereas a metaphor says something *is* something else.

Synonyms

Synonyms are words with the same or similar meanings. For instance, *smart* is a synonym of *intelligent*. However, it is important to note that words with similar meanings often have subtle differences in register or tone. *Purchase* is more formal than *buy*, for instance, while *slim* is a much more positive description than *skinny*.

Special
information

Speech

There are two ways of writing about what someone said:

- In **direct speech**, we repeat the actual words used:

  "There is nothing we can do about it," Mona said.

- In **reported speech** (also called **indirect speech**), we make the words part of our own sentence, usually using a verb such as *say, tell,* or *explain*:

  Mona said that there was nothing we could do about it.

Direct speech

Direct speech is common in fiction and other writing where the actual words of speakers are quoted. The reporting verb (e.g., *say, tell, explain*) may come before the words that were spoken, or after them, or at a natural pause inside the reported sentence:

  Mona said, *"There is nothing we can do about it."*
  "There is nothing we can do about it," **Mona said**.
  "It's no good," **Mona said**, *"We'll just have to ask for help."*

The words spoken must be written inside double quotation marks. In British English, single quotation marks are usually used.

The words spoken always begin with a capital letter as long as the sentence is not divided by a reporting verb. The comma comes inside the quotation marks:

  "Give her a chance," Jamie begged.
  "There is," Mona said, *"nothing we can do about it."*

If the words spoken are a question or an exclamation, there is no comma but instead a question mark or an exclamation point, which comes inside the quotation marks:

> "Why did you do it?" she asked.
> "Oh, mind your own business!" he snapped.

The subject and reporting verb can be used either way around:

> "There is nothing we can do about it," **Mona said**.
> "There is nothing we can do about it," **said Mona**.

> **Tip for success**
> If you are writing a long stretch of direct speech between two characters, it is not always necessary to use reporting verbs each time. As long as it is clear which character is speaking, you can just start a new line within new quotation marks each time a different person speaks.

Reported speech

When you use reported speech, the words put into the reported clause do not exactly match the words actually spoken. For example, you will need to change pronouns, words like *here* and *there*, or the tense of the sentence:

> "I believe **you**."
> She said that she believed **us**.
> "I've been **here** before."
> He said that he had been **there** before.
> "**I've done** the housework."
> He said **he had done** the housework.

Reported speech always has two clauses: the **reported clause**, which contains the words that were spoken, usually in a slightly different

form; and the **main clause**, which contains the reporting verb.
The main clause usually comes first:

> *Katie told me that Marie is going to resign.*
> *Sara asked whether Hardeep was feeling better.*

If the main reported clause is a statement, the main clause is linked to
the reported clause by *that*:

> *Monique said **that** her favorite actor was Ben Kingsley.*
> *John replied **that** he preferred Scarlett Johansson.*

The linking word *that* can be left out after most reporting verbs except
those that mean "answer":

> *She told me **(that)** she was going to leave.*
> *I replied **that** I was very sorry to hear that.*

If the reported clause is a question, the main verb will be a question
word such as *ask, inquire, wonder, query*. The link between the main
clause will be *if* or *whether*:

> *She asked me **if** I was comfortable.*
> *He inquired **whether** the changes had been made.*

Reported clauses can also be used to express what someone is thinking
as well as what is actually spoken:

> *Hussain **wondered** whether **the concert would be sold out**.*
> *Charlotte **thought** that **she had better go and see her family**.*

Key point to remember
Speech in a reported clause is not separated from the reporting
verb by a comma, is not enclosed in quotation marks, and does
not begin with a capital letter unless it is a proper noun.
Reported questions are not followed by question marks.

Questions

There are three main ways of making questions in English:

* With a **question word**, such as *who, why, how*:

    Who *won the race?*
    Which *team was it?*

* With an **auxiliary verb** (*do, have,* or *be*):

    Do *your children like sports?*
    Have *you seen her latest movie?*

* With a modal verb, such as *can* or *may*:

    Can *Mahmoud come too?*
    May *I see the letter?*

Occasionally, we express sentences by our tone of voice, but this would only be appropriate for written English if you are writing direct speech:

    *"**She's left her job?** I thought she was happy there."*

Negative forms of questions almost always use contractions:

    Doesn't *he like talking about his childhood?*
    Can't *Peter have one too?*

If the full *not* form is used, it comes immediately after the subject. The full form is very formal:

    Does *he **not** like talking about his childhood?*
    Can *Peter **not** have one too?*

Questions should always have a question mark at the end, even if they are headings. The only time that a question does not have a question mark is if it is written in reported speech:

> *Do you like cats?*
> *He asked me if I liked cats.*

Sentence tags

Sentence tags look like short questions and are used at the end of sentences. They are sometimes called **question tags**, but many sentences ending with a tag are not real questions.

Tags are usually used to check if the listener or reader agrees with what the speaker or writer has said. Sentence tags are used very commonly in speech and in informal writing such as a chatty email, but rarely in formal written English.

If you need to write them, either in a piece of informal writing, or if you are quoting direct speech, remember that they have a comma before them, and a question mark at the end:

> *You've seen the program, haven't you?*
> *Well, we can't jump over it, can we?*
> *You aren't listening, are you?*

Quotations

There are many reasons to use quotations in your writing:

- To show how the **ideas and research of others** have contributed to your own work.

- To **add evidence** to your arguments, particularly from respected sources.

- To **show different opinions**, sometimes ones that conflict with yours.

- To **add interest or humor** to your writing. If someone has said something particularly clever or witty about your subject, it can liven up your text to quote it.

- In writing about literary works, to give **samples of text for analysis**.

However, do not include too many quotations. You are the author, and your ideas and analysis are the most important part of your writing. Your writing should not rely too heavily on quotations – they should be there to support your work but not to form the main part of it.

Make sure that any quotations you add are there for a good reason – do not put them in simply to make your document longer. Too many quotations can interrupt the flow of your writing and make the text seem cluttered.

Remember that there is a big difference between quoting and **plagiarizing**, which means using the work of others as if it were your own. Even if you use different words rather than quoting directly, if you are using someone else's ideas, you should say so.

Always make sure your quotations are **accurate**. If you have found your quotation as a quotation in someone else's work, you should go back to the original source, if possible, to check it.

It is **not necessary to use whole sentences** in quotes – in fact it is usually best to use only the parts that are relevant to your argument. However, if you take a sentence out of a paragraph, or a word or phrase out of a sentence, make sure that you do not change the author or speaker's intended meaning.

If you use a quote, you must always **explain why you have used it** and what you think its importance is. This can be done very simply. For example, if the quotation clearly backs up a point you have just made, you could use a phrase like:

> *As Dr. X says ...*

Other quotations may need more **analysis and explanation**. You cannot assume that your reader will draw the same conclusions from a quotation as you do, so you must make it very clear what you think its significance is. You might start your next sentence with phrases such as:

> *This shows that ...*
> *[The author] is clearly of the opinion that ...*
> *Put more simply, this means ...*

It is often useful to give a **context** for your quotation, for example, by explaining when and where it was written or spoken, or the situation that the writer or speaker was in.

How to show quotations

For long quotations (around 60 words or more), it is common to use a separate paragraph, indented slightly from the rest of the text and often using a slightly smaller font.

Shorter quotations are usually shown as part of a sentence:

> *Greenberg argued that "the law is the expression of underlying values of culture."*
> *She described the children as "motivated and alert."*

Quotations can also follow an introductory clause, using a colon or a comma before the inverted comma:

> *Charles made a pronouncement: "There will be no more discussion on this matter."*
> *Oscar Wilde once said, "Always forgive your enemies; nothing annoys them so much."*

If you are quoting lines of poetry, you can break the lines as they are in the original poem or show the ends of lines with a slash (/):

> *As an unperfect actor on the stage,/Who with his fear is put beside his part*

If you want to **omit part of a quotation**, you can use an ellipsis inside brackets, like this: [...]

> *She described the play as "racist in a way that was typical of that time, and deeply upsetting."*
> *She described the play as "racist [...] and deeply upsetting."*

If you want to add something to a quotation to make its meaning clearer, put the words you add inside brackets:

> *Giving evidence, the officer said, "I went to his house with Al [Albert Flynn, brother of the accused]."*

If a quotation contains an error, for instance of spelling or grammar, or if it contains something that is surprising, shocking or offensive, and you want to stress that this is *really* what the person said or wrote, use [*sic*], which is Latin for *thus*:

Clarke wrote that he "could of [sic] done it."
(This should be "could have done it.")

Quoting or paraphrasing?

Sometimes you may want to use your own words to explain what someone else has said. This is called paraphrasing. There could be several reasons for this:

- The original quote might be too long, so you need to summarize.
- The original quote might be written in language that is too difficult, so you need to simplify it.
- You might not want to break up your own text with too many direct quotes.
- You need to make a slight change to the original quotation (a verb tense, for example) in order to make it read correctly in your sentence.

Think about the purpose of your quotations. For example, in an essay on literature, it may be necessary to have a lot of quotations so that you can discuss and analyze the actual language of the author. For a science essay, it may be more appropriate to paraphrase most of the ideas you discuss.

If you do paraphrase, you must still make it clear whose work you are using. Make sure that your paraphrase does not change the meaning of the original in any way – if you want to add your own comments, or disagree, you must make it clear which are your ideas and which are the ideas of the person you are paraphrasing.

Referencing quotations

If you use a quotation, you should always say who the speaker or author is, and – if at all possible – what the source was.

This can be done **within the text**, using your own words to introduce the quotation:

> *As Juliet says in Shakespeare's Romeo and Juliet, "Parting is such sweet sorrow."*
> *In a speech during his visit to Berlin in 1963, President John F. Kennedy famously said "Ich bin ein Berliner."*

In **academic writing**, it is usual to refer to a footnote or a bibliography (list of books you used) to reference a quotation. Styles for this can vary, so it is a good idea to ask your teacher if there is a recommended style. A common way is to show the author and the date of the publication in parentheses in the main text, then show the whole source in the bibliography.

In the text:

> *As Prof. Williams points out: "There is a measurable difference between the amount people claim to eat and the amount they actually eat." (Williams, 2007, p. 25)*

In the bibliography:

> Williams, J. (2007) *The Causes of Obesity*. Newtown: Newtown University Press.

If you use a **quotation from a website**, you must reference it in a similar way. Again, there are different styles for this, but a common way is:

> Author, A (date) *Title of article or web page*. Available at: article. com. Accessed on 10/04/2010

Proper nouns

Names of people

Names of people should always begin with capital letters:

> *Ivan Gorecki*
> *Julia Jones*

Titles, such as *Mr.*, *Mrs.*, *Ms.*, *Dr.* are written with periods in American English, but *often* without them in other varieties of English:

> *Ms. Hooper*
> *Prof. McCarthy*

Geographical terms

Remember to use capital letters for all of the following:

- Countries and other political divisions, e.g., *Japan*, *Denver*, *Sierra County*, *Chicago's Pullman neighborhood*, *Halsted Street*
- Nationalities, e.g., *Japanese*, *Swedish*
- Other geographical locations, e.g., *Mount Everest*, *Lake Tahoe*, *the Ohio River*
- Languages, e.g., *French*, *Swahili*

When writing geographical names that begin with *the*, it is more common to use a lower case:

> *the United States*
> *the Alps*

Names of companies and products

Names of companies and products usually have capital letters:

> *Nokia*®
> *Coca-Cola*®

Be careful to spell the name of companies and products exactly as they are spelled by their owners. For instance, the name of the publisher of this book is *HarperCollins*, with no space before the second capital letter.

In formal writing or writing that is to be published, you need to find out if a company name or product name is a registered trademark, and if it is, to put a trademark symbol (® or ™) after the word.

Names of books, plays, movies, etc.

Capital letters are used for the first letter in titles of books, magazines, newspapers, TV shows, movies, etc. Where there are several words, capitals are usually used for the main content words. This means that short prepositions and articles typically begin with a small letter, but longer prepositions and pronouns, even short ones, usually begin with a capital:

> *The Wall Street Journal*
> *The Merchant of Venice*
> *Gone with the Wind*
> *All About My Mother*

If you mention titles such as these in your text, they should be in italic:

> He decided to write a letter to *The Times*.
> Her last book, *Diary of a Wife*, deals with the subject of domestic violence.

The exceptions to this rule are the Bible and the Koran, which remain in ordinary type.

Abbreviations

It can sometimes be difficult to decide when to use periods in abbreviations. In British English, it is becoming more common to use abbreviations without periods, while in American English, they are used more often. In both varieties of English, there are some forms of abbreviation where it is more common to use periods than others.

In some cases, you may make your decision based on the need to avoid ambiguity, e.g., *a.m.* rather than *am*. Make sure that you treat each form consistently throughout your text.

You must be certain that your readers will understand any abbreviations you use. It is safe to use widely understood abbreviations like *NBC* or *FBI*, though even in these cases, if your audience is not American, you may need to add an explanation. However, less common abbreviations could puzzle your readers, so it is best either to avoid them, or to put the full form in parentheses the first time you use them.

There are a few abbreviations that are so widely used that it is not necessary to give the full forms at all. Examples include *USA*, *DNA*, *HIV*, *ATM* and the abbreviations for the main North American time zone designations such as *EDT* and *PST*.

Abbreviations formed from the first letter of all the words can be spelled with or without periods, though it is now more common to omit them:

> *NBC (National Broadcasting Corporation)*
> *FBI (Federal Bureau of Investigation)*

Abbreviations formed from the first part of a word usually need periods:

> *Prof. (Professor)*
> *Oct. (October)*

Abbreviations formed from the first and last letters of a word have a period in American English but usually not in British English:

> St. (street or saint)
> Dr. (doctor)

Abbreviations formed from Latin words use periods:

> e.g. (exempli gratia = for example)
> i.e. (id est = that is to say)
> etc. (et cetera = and the other things)

However, the common Latin abbreviation AD (anno domini = in the year of the lord) and its earlier partner BC (= before Christ) are now more commonly used without periods.

Abbreviations for metric scientific measurements are often formed from the first letter of each of the parts of a compound word. They do not use periods, and you do not add an s to form their plurals:

> kg (**ki**logram or kilograms)
> ml (**m**illiliter or milliliters)

Abbreviations for imperial measurements are often very irregular, and usually have periods. Like metric abbreviations, they do not add s in the plural:

> oz. (ounce or ounces) Comes from the Italian word onza
> lb. (pound or pounds, in weight) Comes from the Latin word libra

Acronyms

Acronyms are words formed from the first letters of several words or from parts of words. If the word is formed only from the first letter of several words, it is properly called an initialism, though most people call these acronyms as well. The difference between acronyms and other abbreviations is that acronyms are pronounced as words themselves, rather than as individual letters:

> NATO (North Atlantic Treaty Organization)
> GUI (graphical user interface)

Acronyms are not usually written with periods. In fact, many acronyms make a journey from being abbreviations to becoming words in their own right. Nobody really thinks of words like laser (Light Amplification by Stimulated Emission of Radiation) or scuba (self contained underwater breathing apparatus) as being abbreviations at all, but they did start out that way.

Numbers

Numbers can be written using figures or letters:

1	*one*
350	*three hundred and fifty*
1,299	*one thousand, two hundred and ninety-nine*

Note that you put a comma or, less usually, a space between each group of three figures, counting from the right:

3,490
2 350 100

In mathematical and scientific writing, numbers are always written as figures. In general writing, you can use words or figures:

480 coulombs is equivalent to 0.005 faradays.
About two hundred people attended the meeting.
We'll need 50 chairs.

It is quite common to use words for numbers less than 10, and figures for larger numbers. Whatever you decide, be consistent throughout your writing.

However, if you have two numbers together, you may use a combination to avoid confusion:

Three 5-year-olds were hurt in a car accident near Lexington.

Very large numbers in the millions, billions or even higher are usually written like this:

40 million
3 billion

Notice that there is no *s* on the end of *million* and *billion* here.

When there has been more than one king or queen with the same name, or sometimes when a man has the same name as his father, grandfather, etc., their names are followed by an ordinal number, usually written in roman numerals:

Henry VIII
George Hamilton IV

Tip for success
Take care with spelling the number *forty* – there is no *u* in it.

Dates

There are several accepted ways of writing dates:

> *June 11, 1961*
> *11 June 1961*
> *6.11.61*
> *06/11/1961*

The style you choose will depend on what you are writing – the longer styles are suitable for essays, polite letters or other formal writing, while the shorter styles are used in quick emails, filling in forms, etc. Note that the American style of writing dates is different from most other countries'. The usual American style is in the order: month – day – year. British English, and many other languages, prefer to use the order: day – month – year.

If you are writing about centuries, the most common style is:

> *During the 15th century ...*

Remember that the name of the century is always the number above the beginning of the years in it, so for instance 1492 is in the 15th century, and 1997 is in the 20th century.

When we are writing about history, the abbreviations *BC* and *AD* are used for dates before and after the birth of Christ.

AH (for Latin *anno Hegirae*, year of the Hegira) designates years in the Muslim calendar. AH 1 is the equivalent of AD 622.

> **Tip for success**
> Note that non-Christian writers often prefer to avoid the abbreviations *BC* and *AD* and use the equivalents *BCE* (*before the common era*) and *CE* (*of the common era*) instead.

Foreign words and phrases

There are many words in English that come from other languages originally, but then become so absorbed into English that we do not think of them as being foreign any more. Examples are *bazaar* from Persian, *karate* from Japanese and *intelligentsia* from Russian. These words are used in just the same way as any other English words.

However, for a word or phrase that is not fully naturalized as English, *italics* are often used:

> The same complaint was repeated *ad nauseam*.
> (Latin = until we were sickened.)
> *Entre nous*, his finances are in a perilous state.
> (French = between ourselves.)
> Her writings displayed a bleak *Weltanschauung*.
> (German = view of life and the world.)

Sometimes it can be difficult to decide if a word has entered mainstream English. If you are unsure whether or not to use italics, consider whether your reader is likely to think of the word or phrase as being part of normal English.

For instance, if you know a lot about yoga, terms such as *chi* (vital energy) and *chakra* (one of the points of physical or spiritual energy) will probably be well known to you. If you are writing for an audience which is also knowledgeable about yoga, you can probably use them without italics and without explanation. However, if your writing is for a general audience, it is best to use italics to indicate that these are words of foreign origin (Chinese and Sanskrit), and also to explain them, at least the first time they are used.

Many foreign words and phrases will only be suitable in very formal or intellectual forms of writing.

Checking
your work

General checks

It is important to **leave time to check your work**, so that the finished quality is as high as possible. Checking falls into two main areas:

• **Overall structure and content**.

• **Detailed points of spelling, grammar, punctuation, etc.**

If you have planned your work carefully and written one or more drafts, as described in the section on Planning in this book, your work should already be logical and well structured. However, even for a short piece of writing, such as a letter or work email, it is worth asking yourself the following questions:

• Has my writing achieved what I wanted it to achieve?
• Have I expressed my points clearly?
• Do my ideas or pieces of information come in a logical sequence?
• Do I have enough evidence to support my points?
• Is the tone of my writing what I wanted it to be?
• Have I included everything I wanted to include?

It can often be a good idea to **ask someone else** to correct your work – your eyes will see what you *intended* to write, whereas someone else may spot errors more easily.

> **Tip for success**
> Many people find it easier to check their work on paper rather than on a computer screen, so if it is important that it is correct, consider printing it out.

Checking spelling

It is important to make sure your spelling is correct. There is a section on spelling in this book that gives general rules, and also a section on words that are often misspelled.

Use your instinct: if a word looks wrong, check it in a dictionary. You can also use a spellchecker on your computer, but make sure that it is set to the variety of English you want: most word processing programs have spelling dictionaries for several varieties of English.

General points to look out for include:

- **Homophones**. These are words that sound the same but are spelled differently, e.g., their/there, witch/which, bare/bear. Remember that the spellchecker on your computer will not be able to find errors in homophones because they are both correct words.

- **Letters that are the wrong way around**. It is very easy to make this kind of error when you are typing your work, for instance typing "form" instead of "from." Since both of these are correct spellings of English words, your spellchecker will not flag them.

- **Missing letters**. Make sure you do not leave out silent letters in words such as *government*, or forget to double the consonant in words such as *swimming*.

> **Tip for success**
> Take particular care with typed writing – it is much easier to make a mistake with fingers on keys than with a pen.

Checking grammar and punctuation

There are sections on grammar and punctuation in this book that give general rules, and also a section on common errors.

General points to look out for include:

- **Apostrophes**. Make sure you have put them in where they are needed and left them out where they are not.

- **Capital letters**. Make sure that all proper nouns have capital letters. It is also a common error to put a lower case "i" where the upper case pronoun "I" is needed.

- **Repeated words**. These are often found at the end of one line and the beginning of another.

- **Missing words**. It can be very easy to leave out little words such as "of" or "in," and equally difficult to spot that they are missing, since your mind can compensate by adding them in unconsciously when you read.

- **Agreement.** This means making sure that all the parts of a sentence relate correctly to each other, avoiding mistakes such as *"We was asked to contribute."* (Should be: *We were asked to contribute.*)

Be especially careful to read sentences that you have changed at some point in your writing. See below under "Checking work written on a computer."

If you are using your computer to write, you will probably have a grammar checker available. This will pick up some common problems, but you should still check your work yourself.

> **Tip for success**
> Do not try to correct huge pieces of text in one go –
> you need to be fresh to be able to spot errors.

Other things to check

- **Facts and information.** If there is any doubt about the source of your information, for instance if it came from a website you are not sure is reliable, make sure you can confirm it in another, more reliable source.

- **Numbers.** Always check numbers, especially long ones such as telephone numbers. It is very easy to make a mistake when you type these.

- **Dates**. If you tell people a meeting is on Thursday the 6th, but the 6th is a Wednesday, you will cause confusion.

- **Repetition of words and phrases**. As you were writing, you may not have realized that you used the same word or phrase over and over again, but when you check at the end – especially if you read your work aloud – you will notice this, and can vary your words if you want to.

- **References**. If you have referred to another book, paper, etc., make sure you have acknowledged it and referenced it properly. In the same way, if you have used charts, diagrams, etc., make sure there are references to them all in the text.

- **Cross-references.** If you have a long document, with many different, numbered sections, you may want to cross-refer from one to another. It is best to do this at the end, when your section headings will not change. If you are writing on a computer, you will be able to set up your document so that cross-references change automatically if the heading numbers change.

Checking work written on a computer

In many ways, computers have made all sorts of writing much easier, especially because we can correct mistakes and move around sections of text without having to write everything out again. However, this also means that it is very easy to introduce mistakes.

If you correct one word in a sentence or one part of a sentence, take great care to make sure that the whole sentence is still correct. For instance, it is very easy to leave in words that are not needed. Look at the following example:

> *She had an important role in his career.*
> *His mother played had an important role in his career.*

The writer only deleted "*she*" instead of "*she had*" when making this correction, leading to an extra verb in the sentence.

Remember, too, to make sure that agreement within a sentence is not affected by a change to part of it:

> *I gave my passport to the officer, who looked at it closely.*
> *I gave my passport and driver's license to the officer, who looked at it closely.*

In this case, the writer has added the words "and driver's license" but has forgotten to change the pronoun *it* later in the sentence to *them*.

Tip for success
If you decide to move a section of text, make sure that you have deleted it from where it was originally.

Marking your corrections

Printing out your work and reading through it on paper can be a helpful way of spotting mistakes. It is usually best to **mark up a whole document or section of a document** on paper before you actually make the changes on the computer. Making each change as you spot it will probably be inefficient and distracting.

When people do **proofreading** in a formal way, there is a set of standard marks that they use. It is unlikely that you will need to learn formal proofreading marks, but some of them can be useful, as they are a clear way of showing your changes, particularly if you are **correcting someone else's writing**.

For example, the mark ^ shows *where* something is to be added, and the text in the margin shows *what* is to be added. The symbol # shows where a space should be added and the symbol ⌐ in the margin indicates that the words in the text with a line through them should be deleted.

There are several books and websites that explain how to use proofreading symbols.

If you are **correcting someone else's work on screen**, it can be useful to use a system that shows the changes you suggest, rather than simply making the changes yourself. That way, an author or editor can decide whether to accept or reject your corrections. You can also leave explanations, comments, and suggestions that another reader can delete later.

Writing

PART TWO

Formal or work emails

Email is much faster than writing letters. You can receive a reply to an email within seconds – or minutes – of sending one. In this way, email is more **like conversation** than paper-based writing. This is its great advantage: email communication, like conversation, can be **two-way** and **almost immediate**. This speed can also be its weakness when people do not take enough care writing emails, especially formal or work emails.

First, here are some general points about email to keep in mind:

- Email tends to be brief.
- Email is generally less formal than communication on paper.
- Email does not communicate emotions as successfully as face-to-face or even telephone conversations. The reader of your email may not be able to tell from your words if you are serious or joking, angry or just surprised.
- Emails, especially very short emails, can sound angry, unfriendly or rude when this is not intended by the writer.

> **Key point to remember**
> Emails that are written very quickly and carelessly can sound unfriendly and rude.

The **rules are less strict** for writing formal or work *emails* than for writing formal *letters*. People have been writing letters for many hundreds of years so rules have had time to develop. Email, as a more recent form of communication, is much less fixed in its rules.

The **rules are** also **different** in different countries and cultures and in different places of work. This point is worth remembering. What is right for one group of people may not be right for all people.

It is also true to say that **everyone** has **their own style** of writing email. Even within the same company, two people may take very different approaches to this form of communication.

The points laid out in this unit are therefore a **guide to writing formal emails**. By following these generally accepted rules, you will get the most out of email. You will also avoid some of the most frequent problems that arise from this form of communication.

> **Tip for success**
> When you join a new company, notice how your colleagues write their emails and consider changing your style to fit in with the company style.

Salutations for formal emails
(Words or phrases used for saying hello)

It is generally a good idea to **start an email with a greeting** rather than beginning the message immediately. Just like a face-to-face exchange of greetings, email greetings:

- show that you are friendly and pleasant
- show respect for the reader

In addition, a greeting allows the reader to pause for a moment before reading the message itself.

If, however, you and a colleague are writing a series of short emails to each other on a particular subject, the rules are different. It is generally acceptable after the first exchange of emails to include only the information, without greetings.

Note that if you are using **instant messaging**, which is an even faster method of communication, you only need to add a salutation to the first in a series of messages that you send to someone.

There are no fixed rules for the type of greeting that you use. Generally, if you are emailing someone that you work with or even someone that you do not know, it is acceptable to **start the email** with a simple "**Hello**" or "**Hello James.**" (If you know the colleague well, "**Hi**" or "**Hi James**" might also be fine.)

You may want to **show more respect** in your greeting, perhaps if the person is much older than you, has a higher rank than you in the same company, or is from a country or culture that is more formal than yours. If you are in any doubt about this, you could address the person, "**Dear Mr. Sanchez**" or "**Dear Ms. Sanchez.**"

If you receive an email and the sender of the message has used his or her first name only, it is **acceptable to use their first name** when you reply.

> **Key point to remember**
> If you decide to use the more formal salutation "Dear Mr. Sanchez" or "Dear Ms. Sanchez," make sure that you use the correct title. If the person you are emailing is a doctor, for example, be sure to include that in the salutation.

Subject lines

People who use email for work often complain that they receive too much email and that it takes up too much of their time dealing with it.

You can help with this situation by **making full use of the subject line**. The subject line gives you the chance to tell the reader of your email **why you are emailing them** before they have even opened your message.

For example, if you are emailing a company to ask for information about a product, in the subject line, write the name of the product and the fact that you need information:

> *Subject: Balance bike (ref: N765) info required*

The subject line gives you the chance to **show the main points** of your email. If you start to type "Hi" or "Another thing" in the subject line, think for a moment whether you can replace it with something more useful.

Look at the following subject lines and see how, in only a few words, you can show the main points of an email:

> *Subject: Meeting Room changed to 307*

> *Subject: Lunch (Fri 9 Oct) canceled*

> *Subject: REQ: Feb sales figures*

> *Subject: Reminder: conference agenda due*

Tip for Success
Write a useful subject line that says in just a few words what your email is about and what, if any, action you need the reader to take.

Content and length

Before you even start to type your message, make sure you can answer the following two questions:

- Why am I writing this?
- What do I want the reader of this email to do?

Remember that most people receive a lot of email in the course of a working day. For this reason, they do not welcome long emails! Your job is therefore to **tell them your point or points quickly and clearly**. Here are a few tips to help you do this:

- Make the first sentence count. Introduce the topic of the email clearly and in a few words.

- Write in short paragraphs. Separate paragraphs, each relating to a different point, will make the information easier to understand. Do not allow important points to get lost in one long paragraph.

- Consider using headings within the body of your message if the message relates to several different subjects.

- Consider numbering your points. The reader will find this useful when responding to particular points.

- Leave a space between each paragraph.

- Use short sentences. Try to keep your sentences to a maximum of 20 words. These can be quickly read and understood.

- If possible, try to fit your message onto one screen so that the reader does not have to scroll down to see the rest of it.

Read the following email. Consider:

- Is the information presented in the clearest way?

- Did the writer think about the needs of the reader as she wrote her email?

Subject: conference dinner
From: "Hill, Lucy" <Lucy.Hill@bigbooks.co.uk>
To: "Ollie Walsh"

Hi Ollie

Thanks again for offering to help out with the arrangements for the conference dinner. I appreciate it. I met with David yesterday to finalize details and here's what we decided: The venue (Carmichael Hall) is reserved for Dec 18th, 7:00–12:00. Your contact there is Julia Winters (354 638-9761). Invitations should go out to all conference delegates the week starting November 3rd. The invitations are currently with the printers, btw, and when they are returned to us (this Friday) will need checking against the original delegate list which I'll get Sujata to send to you. Hallidays, the caterers, will need to know final numbers by Dec. 10th at the latest. Please call them to let them know. Last, could you please check with Sujata over the timing of the speeches and let the relevant people know when their slot is.

Many thanks,
Lucy

Now see how much clearer the same message looks when the writer considers what will be most helpful to the reader and has:

- broken the text up into separate, short paragraphs

- given each paragraph a heading

- allowed plenty of white space

Subject: conference dinner
From: "Hill, Lucy" <Lucy.Hill@bigbooks.com>
To: "Ollie Walsh"

Hi Ollie

Thanks again for offering to help out with the arrangements for the conference dinner. I appreciate it. I met with David yesterday to finalize details and here's what we decided:

Venue
The venue (Carmichael Hall) is reserved for Dec 18th, 7:00–12:00. Your contact there is Julia Winters (354 638-9761)

Invitations
The invitations are currently with the printers. When they are returned to us (this Friday) they will need checking against the original delegate list, which I'll get Sujata to send to you. Invitations should go out to all conference delegates the week starting November 3rd.

The caterers
Hallidays, the caterers, will need to know final numbers by Dec. 10th. Please call them to let them know.

Speeches
Last of all, could you please check with Sujata over the timing of the speeches and let the relevant people know when their slot is.

Many thanks,
Lucy

Tone

Read the following email and ask yourself how the writer was feeling when he wrote it:

Subject: conference dinner
From: "Walsh, Ollie" <Ollie.Walsh@bigbooks.com>
To: "Lucy Hill"

Lucy,

There are problems re the arrangements for the conference dinner:

1. The invitations just arrived this morning so I will be late sending them out.

2. Julia Winters called late yesterday. She was under the impression that 150 people were attending. Sujata's list says it's 170. Which of these is right?

3. Re the speeches, Alice and David are fine with 10 minutes each but Michael wants 15 minutes. Is he allowed 15 minutes? Also, you didn't ask Sandra to speak and she's offended. Did you mean not to ask her or is this an oversight?

Ollie

Perhaps the writer of this email was angry or stressed. That is certainly the impression that his email gives. However, it is possible that he was neither angry not stressed: he simply needed advice from Lucy about how to act. Supposing he was not angry, how might he have written exactly the same questions but in a polite and pleasant way?

Now compare the tone of the previous email with this email:

Dear Lucy,

I'm afraid[1] there are a few problems re the arrangements for the conference dinner: (This shouldn't make too much difference.[2])

1. FYI, the invitations only arrived this morning so I'm afraid I will be a day late sending them out.

2. Julia Winters called late yesterday. She was under the impression that 150 people were attending. Sujata's list says it's 170. Do you know[3] which of these figures is right?

3. Re the speeches, Alice and David are fine with 10 minutes each but Michael would prefer[4] 15 minutes. Is this possible? Also, I have heard that Sandra Winters would like to speak too. This may not be possible but I thought I'd let you know.[5]

Best,
Ollie

Here the writer explains the same problems and asks the same questions without making the reader feel that the problems are all her fault. Notice how:

[1] Before he tells her about a problem, he writes "I'm afraid ..."
[2] He tells her about a problem but lets her know that it is not serious.
[3] He adds "Do you know" to the question, which softens it.
[4] He uses the polite phrase "would prefer" rather than the direct verb "wants."
[5] In the first version of the email he blames the reader (you didn't ask Sandra to speak and she's offended). Here, he simply lets the reader know that there is a problem. She can then decide what to do.

Generally, people intend their emails to be **polite and pleasant** – or at least neutral. However, because emails are often brief and quickly written, they can sometimes sound slightly demanding, angry, or even rude.

Remember that the reader of your email **cannot see you smile** and **cannot hear that your voice is friendly**. Try to be aware of this potential problem and to develop ways of showing that you are polite and friendly through the words that you write. This is *especially* true if the person you are emailing has never met you.

If you are emailing someone that you have spoken or written to before, consider starting your message by saying "**I hope you are well**." Again, this lets the reader know that you are friendly and pleasant.

It is fine to keep your emails brief, but **not too brief**. You want to communicate quickly and efficiently but you still need to show respect to the reader and to show that you have considered their feelings. This can be difficult, especially when you are in a hurry, but it is important. If, for example, you are giving a piece of bad news, start your sentence with "I'm afraid ..." or "I'm sorry ..." rather than just stating the problem.

Be aware that verbs used in **the passive can sound a little formal**. For example "The sales report that you were sent in February" (passive) sounds slightly formal (whereas "the sales report that I sent you in February" (active) does not). This is fine if you want to write a slightly formal email. If you are emailing a colleague that you know well, and want to write a friendlier email, however, you may want to avoid this structure.

Do not write using all UPPER-CASE LETTERS. People sometimes use upper-case letters to show the difference between their own writing and someone else's. This may make the reader think that you are angry and shouting. Upper-case letters are also more difficult to read than lower-case letters.

Always read an email that you have written before you send it, especially if you are writing to disagree with someone. **Imagine that you are the reader** and try to **read the email as they will read it**. Does it sound angry, aggressive, or demanding and, if so, is that *really* what you intended? If you are in any doubt, do not send the email immediately. Save it and read it later in the day when you are feeling calm and can judge whether you need to change it.

> **Tip for success**
> Before you send an email, read it to check that the tone of it is what you intended.

Punctuation and abbreviations

Generally, the rules for spelling, grammar, and punctuation that apply to letter-writing also apply to formal or work emails:

- Bad spelling, grammar, and punctuation may give the reader a bad opinion of you and of your company, if you work for one.
- In addition, they may make your message unclear or confusing. In particular, emails that lack periods or commas are difficult to read.

It is generally agreed that **contractions** (I'm, he's, can't, etc.) **are acceptable** in most formal or work emails. In formal *letters*, the full form of the words should be used but, as we have said before, formal emails are less formal than formal letters.

Other abbreviations, such as "U" for "you," "plz" for "please," and "thx" for "thanks," though often used in personal email, are generally not acceptable in formal or work emails.

Likewise, emoticons or smileys ☺ are not generally used in formal or work emails:

- They are considered too informal or familiar.

- There is a risk that the reader will not understand what you mean by these symbols.

> **Tip for success**
> Always read an email before you send it, to check for errors.

Ending a formal email

Between the main part of the email and the signoff, (the part that says goodbye), there is often a line linking the two.

What you write at this point will, of course, depend on the purpose of your email, but here are a few typical sentences that are often used:

- *I hope to hear from you soon.*
- *I look forward to hearing from you.*
- *I look forward to your response.*
- *Many thanks for your time.*
- *Thanks again for this.*
- *Many thanks in advance.*
- *Thank you for taking the time to answer my questions.*
- *I hope this helps.*
- *Please get in touch if you have any more queries.*
- *Please do not hesitate to get in touch if you have any questions.*
- *Let me know what you think.*

Just as it is a good idea to start an email with a greeting, it is also **polite to finish an email with a signoff**. Not everyone does this: some people end an email by typing their name alone. But an email that ends without a signoff can sound a little rude, especially if the content of the email has included a disagreement or problem.

A number of signoffs are commonly used in formal or work emails. Again, there are no fixed rules for the type of signoff that you use. The phrases below are some of the most common.

- *Many thanks*
- *Thank you*
- *Thanks again*
- *Best*
- *Regards*
- *Best regards*
- *Kind regards*
- *Warm regards*
- *Best wishes*
- *With best wishes*

Below is an example of a slightly formal email. The sender of the email (an artist), is replying to a person who has made an enquiry about her work. They have never met each other. Notice the tone, which is polite and friendly but still slightly formal.

Subject: paintings
From: "Lewis, Lara" <lara.lewis@macp.com>
To: "Michael Peters"

Hello Michael,

Thank you for your inquiry.

I am a studio artist at Multnomah Arts Center in Portland. You are welcome to visit me there anytime and have a look at the paintings I have available (no obligation of course!).

I also attend events around the country as you can see in the 2010 Events page on my website.

Prices start at $250 for the small paintings (approx. 8" x 12"). The larger paintings are about $600 (12" x 15") depending on the piece.

I also undertake commissions if you have something specific in mind.

Please give me a call on (503) 459-8253 if you would like to come to my studio and we can arrange a suitable time.

Kind regards,
Lara

This email is sent from one colleague to another. This time, as the sender and reader know each other, the tone is slightly less formal, though it is still formal enough to be suitable for work.

Subject: minutes (meeting 03/20/10)
From: "Rose, Andrew" <andrew.rose@wentworths.com>
To: "Helena Ghiotto"

Hi Helena,

I'm attaching the minutes from yesterday's meeting.

Thanks very much for coming to the meeting. I think we all found it very useful to have your sales perspective on the various issues. Sophia and I agreed that it would be good to have you or Chris present at such meetings in the future. Perhaps we could discuss this over coffee sometime?

Would you mind emailing me a copy of Jeanne's report? Thanks in advance.

Have a good trip – and please say hi to Carlo from me.

Best,
Andrew

Informal or social emails

The rules for writing informal or social emails are very relaxed. Generally, when people email their friends, **they write as they speak**. They use the same words as they would use in speech and they put those words together in much the same way.

Salutations

(Words or phrases used for saying hello, also called greetings.)

People generally **start informal emails with a greeting** in order to sound friendly. There are no fixed rules for the type of greeting used. Generally, people write "**Hi**" or "**Hi Julia**" or "**Hello**" or "**Hello Julia**." Sometimes there is no greeting and the name of the reader alone is used.

Tone

As we have said before, email does not communicate emotions very clearly. The reader of an email cannot see the sender's face or hear their voice and they may struggle to work out how they are feeling. This is especially true when an email has been written very quickly or with little care. One solution to this problem is the **smiley** or **emoticon**, a typed symbol representing a face. Smileys are used either to show how the sender feels or to show the tone of an email when the words alone do not make this clear. The most common of these smileys are shown below:

☺ or ☻	I am happy/pleased/friendly.
☹ or ☺	I am sad, disappointed, or fed up.
☺	I am enthusiastic/eager.
☺	I am surprised or shocked.
☺	I am joking/being sarcastic.

Punctuation and abbreviations

Some people take care to punctuate their informal emails correctly but many do not. For example, it is quite common to see informal emails written completely in lower-case letters. Generally, people do not expect perfect punctuation in this type of email.

Emails **often include abbreviations**. Some of the most common abbreviations are shown below. It is worth remembering when you use one of these that not everyone knows what all these abbreviations mean.

AFAIK	As Far As I Know	IMHO	In My Humble Opinion
AKA	Also Known As	IOW	In Other Words
ASAP	As Soon As Possible	IRL	In Real Life
B4	Before	L8R	Later
BTW	By The Way	LOL	Laughing Out Loud
CUL8R	See You Later	NSFW	Not Safe For Work
CYA	See Ya	OTOH	On The Other Hand
CYU	See You	POV	Point Of View
FWIW	For What It's Worth	ROTFL	Rolling On The Floor Laughing
FYA	For Your Amusement	TAFN	That's All For Now
FYI	For Your Information	TIA	Thanks In Advance
HTH	Hope This Helps	TTYL	Talk To You Later
IGWS	It Goes Without Saying	TTFN	Ta Ta For Now
IMO	In My Opinion	THX	Thanks

Ending an informal email

As with email openings, there are no fixed rules for how to end informal emails. In a very quickly written email there may be no signoff (the part before the name that says goodbye), or just the name of the sender. Sometimes, people write only the first letter of their name instead of their whole name. However, **most people like to use a signoff** because it is friendly. Additionally, between the main part of the email and the signoff, there is often an extra line linking the two. Below are some examples:

- *Talk to you later.*
- *Hope you're doing okay/well.*
- *Hope you're all well.*
- *See you soon.*
- *Better go now.*
- *Tell you more when we speak.*
- *Have a good weekend.*
- *Hope to see you soon.*

A number of signoffs are commonly used in informal emails before the name of the sender. The phrases below are some of the most frequent:

- *Love*
- *Lots of love*
- *Take care*
- *Ciao*
- *Later*
- *See you*
- *See ya!*
- *Cheers!*

Text messages

Texting (more formally, text messaging) between cell phones is an extremely popular form of communication. Its great advantage is that it allows people to communicate almost as quickly as spoken language in situations where speech is not suitable.

Text messages (or informally, texts) are **short** as there is a limit to the number of characters that can be used in each message. Because of this, a special language of **text abbreviations** has developed. Some of these abbreviations include numbers as well as letters. Here are some of the most common text abbreviations with their meanings:

@	at	gr8	great	tx/thx	thanks
2	to, too or two	ic	I see	u	you
2day	today	l8	late	w8	wait
2moro	tomorrow	l8r	later	wan2	want to
4	for	lo	hello	wk	week
aml	all my love	m8	mate	wrk	work
b4	before	pls	please	xlnt	excellent
btw	by the way	r	are	y	why
c	see	some1	someone		
cm	call me	spk	speak		
cu	see you	sry	sorry		
cul	see you later	syl	see you later		

Sometimes people also use **smileys** or **emoticons** in their texts. These are typed symbols representing a face, as shown in the previous section under "Tone."

Formal or work letters

Nowadays so much communication is done through email and the telephone that the skill of formal letter writing can get forgotten. However, letters are still used in some situations.

Here is a general layout for a formal letter. Note that the layout of formal letters varies but that this format is generally accepted.

---

[1]**Anthony Johnson**

5130 Molden Road
Waldorf MD 20601

Phone 410 360 5625
Cell 443 532 5437
E-mail tonyrjohnson@lycos.com

[2]November 18, 2010

[3]Ms. Harriet Jones
Planning Officer
St. Mary's County Planning Board
Waldorf MD 20601

[4]Dear Ms. Jones:

[5]**Planning Application Ref. No. 09/291/XUL**

Thank you for your letter informing us of this application. As the owners and occupiers of 5130 Molden Road, we are concerned that the building of five new houses will create an unacceptable degree of noise and disturbance in the area.

We are also anxious about the amount of traffic that this development will generate. As parents who cycle on Molden Road with our children, we feel that the extra volume of traffic will make the road unsafe.

For these reasons, we believe that this is a highly unsuitable proposal for development in this area, and hope that the Zoning Board will reject the application.

[6]Yours sincerely,

Anthony Johnson   *Sylvie Johnson*

[7]Mr. Anthony & Mrs. Sylvie Johnson

1. Most people today write letters on letterhead, which is special stationery that shows the sender's name and address. Companies use professionally printed letterhead with their logo and other information on it. Computer programs have templates that make it easy for you to create your own personal letterhead. If you do not use letterhead, you can write your address at the top of the letter.

2. Write the date on the left, under the letterhead. Write the month in full as a word.

3. Write the address of the person that you are writing to on the left, under the date.

4. If you know the name of the person you are writing to, use a courtesy title and the family name to address them. If you do not know the name of the person you are writing to, write "Dear Sir or Madam." In a business letter you normally use a colon after this line; in other kinds of letters, a comma is preferred.

5. The heading goes here in bold, giving the subject matter of the letter. This will not be appropriate for all formal letters but it is useful in cases where the letter clearly relates to a particular subject.

6. Write "Yours sincerely," "Sincerely yours," or just "Sincerely" at the end of the letter. Remember to start the first word with a capital letter.

7. Write your signature by hand and then type your name under it. Put your given name first and family name second.

> **Key point to remember**
> If you know that the person you are sending the letter to is a woman but you do not know how she prefers to be addressed, use the title, Ms. Ms. is used for both married and single women.

Most formal letters have a similar structure, having an introduction, a main part and a conclusion.

In your first paragraph, introduce the reason that you are writing. This should be brief – a line or two is usually enough.

> *On June 20th, 2009, I bought a self-assembly children's scooter (model: XR36) from you for $40 which I paid for with cash.*

In the main part of the letter **give details which explain the reason that you are writing**. Keep this as brief as you can. Say everything that you need to say but no more. Present the facts in a logical order that can easily be understood.

> *The next day I unpacked and assembled the scooter and my son rode it to the park. After half an hour of using the scooter, I noticed that the middle of the rear wheel was cracked. I immediately stopped my son from riding on the scooter as I was worried that it was unsafe.*

In the conclusion to your letter, **tell the reader what you would like them to do** as a result of your letter:

> *I am not at all happy with the quality of this scooter and am therefore requesting a full refund.*

The language that you use in a formal letter must be appropriate. It should be polite, whatever subject you are writing about. It does not need to be very formal but it **must not be *informal***. Therefore, you should:

- avoid slang or informal language
- avoid contractions, such as *I'm, he's, they've,* etc.

Make sure that you **spell the name of the person that you are writing to correctly**. People can feel offended when their names are misspelled.

It is helpful to **write a clear heading** before the main part of your letter. This tells the reader exactly what the letter is about. There is a greater chance that the reader will pay attention to your letter if they know from the start what they are dealing with.

Take care over the appearance of your letter. Present the text in short blocks and leave plenty of white space between them. Prepare a letter that looks easy to read.

If at all possible, make your letter no longer than one page. People who have to deal with many letters are much more likely to deal immediately with a letter that is simple, short, and to the point.

> **Key point to remember**
> Make sure that you use the reader's correct title. For example, do not write *Mr. ...*' if the reader has some other more specific title that is appropriate, such as *Dr.* or *Prof.*

When you are planning your letter, try to **think of the contents of that letter from the point of view of the reader**. Most working people read a great deal of text every day, whether it is email, text messages or printed matter. Most people are also very busy in their jobs and have only a limited amount of time to read a message in whatever form it is sent.

You – the letter writer – must therefore try to help the reader by making the message of the letter as clear as possible. You can do this by:

- giving the main point (or points) first. Your reader will immediately want to know why you are writing to them and may feel impatient with your letter if they have to read through a lot of text in order to find this out.

- not including too much information. Only write what the reader needs to know. Do not include a lot of details or the reader may struggle to understand the main point of the letter.

- not including irrelevant information. This might confuse the reader or make them impatient.

- keeping your sentences short and simple. Short sentences with a simple structure are easier to understand.

Tip for success
Write a clear letter that can be easily understood, no longer than one page if possible.

Look at this letter written by the parent of a child to the child's teacher:

362 Maple Street
Hanover, PA 17331

13 December 2010

West Manheim Elementary School
670 Baltimore Street
Hanover, PA 17331

Dear Ms. Lennon,

I am writing to clarify the situation regarding Millie's nut allergy as I know this has recently caused some confusion and concern. Millie has a slight allergy to almonds and hazelnuts. The allergy is mild and not life-threatening but it does cause swelling of the mouth, which Millie finds distressing. Our doctor has recommended that Millie avoids eating all foods containing these nuts. If any of the children brings birthday cake or cookies to school, could Millie please not be given any in case the food sets off an allergic reaction. In the event of Millie accidentally eating food that contains almonds or hazelnuts, please administer the medicine that the school nurse now has in her office. This will immediately alleviate the symptoms. The medicine is clearly marked with Millie's name. I hope this clarifies the situation. If you have any questions, please call me at (717) 729-3045. Many thanks for your help.

Yours sincerely,
Anna Green

Now see how much clearer and easier to read the letter is when:

- a heading is used, giving the reason for the letter
- the text is broken up into short paragraphs
- there is plenty of white space around those paragraphs

362 Maple Street
Hanover, PA 17331

13 December 2010

West Manheim Elementary School
670 Baltimore Street
Hanover, PA 17331

Dear Ms. Lennon,

Millie Green's nut allergy

I am writing to clarify the situation regarding Millie's nut allergy as I know this has recently caused some confusion and concern.

Millie has a slight allergy to almonds and hazelnuts. The allergy is mild and not life-threatening but it does cause swelling of the mouth, which Millie finds distressing. Our doctor has recommended that Millie avoids eating all foods containing these nuts.

If any of the children brings birthday cake or cookies to school, could Millie please not be given any in case the food sets off an allergic reaction.

In the event of Millie accidentally eating food that contains almonds or hazelnuts, please administer the medicine that the school nurse now has in her office. This will immediately alleviate the symptoms. The medicine is clearly marked with Millie's name.

I hope this clarifies the situation. If you have any questions, please call me at (717) 729-3045.

Many thanks for your help.

Yours sincerely,
Anna Green

Letters of complaint

Letters are sometimes written to make complaints, for example, about the quality of goods or services. The following letter is written by a woman who is unhappy with the service that she recently received in a restaurant:

Carla Sylva
1452 Calle Amapolas Apt 103
Carolina PR 00979-1126

Phone 939 384 6937
Cell 939 382 6021
E-mail csylva@Yahoo.com

17 June 2010

Maria's
Urb Las Gladiolas
150 Calle A
San Juan PR 00926

Dear Sir or Madam:

[1] I am writing to complain about the poor service I received in your restaurant, where my friend and I had lunch last Saturday (June 13th).

[2] Having requested over the phone a table by the window, we were disappointed to find ourselves seated instead at the back of the restaurant. Our food took over an hour to come and when it arrived, my friend's main course was cold. We complained about this and our waitress returned the food to the kitchen for reheating. Unfortunately, she forgot to bring the food back to us and, when we reminded her, she was discourteous. Neither dessert that we chose from the menu was available and, although we asked for our coffee to arrive with dessert, it came ten minutes later.

[3] As a result of all this, we did not enjoy our meal. Your restaurant had been recommended to us by a friend but we were extremely disappointed by what we found.

[4] I am enclosing a copy of the bill and would like to receive a refund of at least half of it.

I look forward to hearing from you soon.

Yours faithfully,

Carla Sylva.

Carla Sylva

---

1 In the opening paragraph, explain briefly what you are complaining about.
2 In the main paragraph explain the problem, giving particular examples of what you are dissatisfied with. Include relevant details, such as dates and places. Give enough information here but not so much that the important parts are lost.
3 Tell the reader what the result of all these problems was.
4 Tell the reader what you would like them to do about the problem.

Be polite. Keep the tone of your letter polite and as pleasant as possible. You may feel that the reader is to blame for your situation but do not be rude because of this. If the reader is offended by what you write, he or she will probably not want to help you with your problem. In any case, the person reading your letter will probably not have caused your problem.

Stay calm. You may be angry but try not to let this show. Never use an aggressive or insulting tone. Avoid adjectives such as "terrible" and "appalling" that cause or show strong emotion; use calmer, more neutral words instead. If you are obviously angry in your letter, it will probably make the person reading it not at all enthusiastic about helping you.

Job-related letters

People often apply for a job by sending their résumé to a company, together with a job application letter, which is often called a cover letter. With a well-written cover letter you can:

- point out the most important parts of your résumé

- show a potential employer that you can write effectively

- show a potential employer that you are a pleasant person

2nd floor, OKW Osaka Bldg,
1-6-2 Awajimachi, Chuo-ku,
Osaka 541-0047

18 October 2010

Ms. Helena Sano
10th floor, Sakae East Bldg,
4-2-7 Sakae, Naka-ku,
Nagoya 460-0008

Dear Ms. Sano:

[1] **RE: Editorial assistant**

[2] I am writing to apply for the above post as advertised in the Evening Sun on October 16. I am enclosing my résumé, as requested.

[3] I am currently working in a publishing company that specializes in children's books. [4] I have been working on various aspects of publishing, including editing, in cooperation with freelance editors and checking manuscripts.

I have worked in this company for two years and have gained considerable experience and knowledge. [5] I now feel that it is time to take my career to the next step. I am looking for a position that will provide new challenges and engage me more fully in the publishing process. [6] I am organized and energetic and I enjoy meeting and working with a range of people.

[7] I would welcome the opportunity to discuss my skills and experience with you.

I look forward to hearing from you.

Yours sincerely,

Thomas Maruako

Thomas Maruako

1   Give the title of the job that you are applying for here.
2   Give details of the job that you are applying for and say how you found out about it.
3   Describe the job that you are doing now, including details of tasks and responsibilities.
4   Tell the reader what skills and knowledge you have gained in your current job.
5   Tell the reader why you want to leave your current job for the new job.
6   Describe the qualities that make you suitable for the new job.
7   Say that you would be pleased to provide the reader with more information.

Do not write too much in your cover letter. The main part of the letter should have two or three short paragraphs only. Ideally, the whole letter should fit on one page.

Write a cover letter for each new job that you apply for. Do not assume that a general letter will be enough. Write specifically about the job that you are applying for and keep in mind the skills and qualities that are right for that job.

Tip for success
Always address a cover letter to a particular person.
If you know the title of their job but not the person's name, call the company and ask for the name.

The following is a letter of inquiry, written by a person who is looking for work. It is not a response to a job advertisement. Instead it is the sort of letter that a person who wants work sends to several potential employers, hoping that one of them will require their services:

Sophia Pylas
3 Victoria Street
Wellington 6011

6 August 2010

Hotel Grand
26 Quay Street
Auckland 1021
BR2 4UT

Dear Sir or Madam:

I am writing to inquire about the possibility of work in your hotel this summer. I am especially interested in reception duties but would seriously consider any other type of work that you could offer me.

I am a twenty-year-old student and for the last three years have spent every summer working in hotels in Wellington. I have worked as a receptionist, a waitress and a cleaner. This summer I intend staying with relations in Auckland from December 5th till January 31st and am hoping to find employment for this period.

I enclose a résumé giving details of my work experience and very much look forward to hearing from you.

With thanks

Yours faithfully

Sophia Pylas

Sophia Pylas

Informal letters

Again, so much communication is done through email and the telephone these days that informal letters between friends are becoming quite rare. Still, some people like to write letters – or at least notes – to their friends. There are also some occasions when, even between good friends, a letter seems more appropriate than an email.

---

[1] *December 18th, 2010*

[2] *Dear Sara,*

[3] *It was great to speak to you last week – thanks for calling. I'm so sorry I haven't been in touch this year. It's been quite hectic with one thing and another!*

[4] *We're both really excited that you're coming to see us in the new year – it's been far too long. I just thought I'd better remind you to bring your hiking shoes. There are some fantastic walks we can do around here (if we have the energy!) Also, make sure you bring warm sweaters and coats. The scenery here is gorgeous but it is <u>very</u> cold, especially in January (and I seem to remember from our college days that you feel the cold!)*

Did I mention I bumped into Steve Washington in Albany earlier this year? He looked so different I almost didn't recognize him. Anyway, I'll tell you more when I see you …

[5] *Really looking forward to seeing you both. I'll call you nearer the time with directions.*

[6] *Much love,*
Emma [7] *xxx*

[8] *P.S. Can't wait to see you with short hair!*

¹ You do not need to write your address here, although some people do. If you want to give the reader a new or different address, you can write it here. If you sometimes write from one place and sometimes another, you may show which of these addresses you are writing from by putting, for example:

> *Chicago*
> *December 18th, 2010*

² You can use the traditional greeting for an informal letter, which is "Dear Paolo/Greta, etc." or you may like to write simply, "Hi Paolo/Greta, etc.," followed by a comma.

³ You can start an informal letter by referring to a previous communication with the reader. You can also start by asking about the health of the reader or by saying sorry for not having written to or telephoned the reader recently:

- *How are you?*
- *How are you doing?*
- *I hope you're both well.*
- *I'm sorry it's been so long since my last letter.*

⁴ The tone of an informal letter is very often conversational. Just as in conversation, you can use informal words and phrases freely. You can use contractions (e.g., *I'm*, *won't*, etc) too and you do not have to write in full sentences.

⁵ You can end a letter by saying how pleased you are that you are going to see the reader soon. You may also encourage the reader to write or to call you:

- *It'll be great to see you.*
- *It would be great to meet up one of these days.*
- *Can't wait to see you.*

- *Hope to hear from you soon.*
- *Stay in touch.*
- *Write soon.*

6   If you are writing to a close friend, before you sign your name, you will want to show affection by using a word or phrase such as:

- *Love,*
- *Lots of love,*
- *Much love,*
- *All my love,*
- *Love from,*

If you are writing to a friend that you do not know so well, you may prefer:

- *Best wishes,*
- *All the best,*
- *Kind regards,*
- *Regards,*

7   If you are very close to the reader, you can add a kiss or kisses after your name (x or xxx) or a hug or hugs (o or ooo).

8   If, when you have finished writing your letter, you think of something else that you want to add, you can put it after the letters, "P.S." (an abbreviation for post script).

Letters are still sometimes written to mark special occasions. For example, here is a letter congratulating the reader on getting a new job:

Mexico City
July 3rd

Hi Channa,

How are you doing? I'm just dropping you a line because I wanted to say congratulations on landing your exciting new job!

Norberto and I are both very pleased for you. You told us last time we met up that you were looking around but didn't seem very optimistic about the opportunities. I know there are a lot of people out there chasing not many jobs. You must have been pretty impressive in interview!

Anyway, I just wanted to congratulate you. I hope the job is everything you want it to be and that you get to work with a great bunch of people.

Well done, Channa!

Lots of love, Marta and Norberto

Notice that the letter, though informal, follows the basic structure for formal letters. It has:

- an introduction, where the writer says why she is writing the letter, i.e., to congratulate the reader on getting her job
- a main part, where the writer puts background information, writing that she knew the reader was looking for a new job and that she knew finding work was difficult
- a conclusion, where the writer congratulates the reader again and adds two specific wishes of her own

Another occasion which often makes people feel that they should write letters is the death of a person loved by the reader. People often feel that the seriousness of the occasion deserves a proper letter and not a quickly written email. A letter, rather than a phone call, also gives the writer time to think about what they want to say and how they are going to say it. This can be a very hard letter to write.

San Diego
June 13, 2010

Dear Polly,

I'm writing because I've just heard the very sad news about your Dad. I just wanted to tell you how sorry I am and to let you know that I am thinking of you.

I have very fond memories of Colin. He was a very kind, warm man and always so welcoming when I came to visit. You enjoyed such a good relationship with him and remained so close throughout your adult life. I know you will be devastated by his death. I am very sorry. I know Ben will be a great comfort to you at this difficult time.

Thinking of you, Polly, and sending you all my love.

Julia

Again, this letter follows the introduction – main part – conclusion format.

- An introduction, where the writer says that she has been told that the person has died.
- A main part, where the writer relates good memories of the dead person and says they know how important the person was to the reader. This part also often includes something that the writer hopes will comfort the reader.
- A conclusion, where the writer usually says that they are thinking of the reader.

Blogs

A blog is a website where someone regularly writes their thoughts and opinions in the form of a *post*, that is, a text that appears all at one time – often daily. Blogs usually contain text, images and links to other websites.

Blogs are written for various reasons. Many people write blogs in order to comment on political issues or stories in the news. Some bloggers write about particular activities and all the issues that relate to them, while other people write blogs in order to sell a product or service. Some blogs, meanwhile, just describe what the blogger does in daily life.

The style and tone of a blog will depend very much on its content. A cycling blog written by an avid cyclist might have an informative and factual tone. The blog writer (*blogger*) wants to provide useful information for other cyclists and to share experiences with them. They may not be so interested in entertaining their readers.

A political blog, on the other hand, might be very funny, using humor in order to criticize politicians.

The blog that someone writes about their daily life will probably have an informal tone and be written in the style of a conversation, chatting to readers as if they were friends.

Whatever the content or subject matter of the blog that you are writing, there are a few general rules.

The first – and possibly the most important – is to **consider your reader**. **Who** do you intend to read this? What are their interests and opinions, and **what do they want from your blog**? Do they want:

- information on a particular subject?
- entertainment?
- to hear your opinions?
- all of the above?

It is only by providing what your reader wants that you will keep them coming back for more.

It might help to **think of your blog as a *resource*** for the reader. For example, if you are writing a blog about a particular sport, you might like to **share tips** with the reader about techniques that you have discovered that have improved your performance. Or you might **provide links** to websites that sell equipment that you have found useful. Give your reader the advantages of your experience and knowledge.

> **Key point to remember**
> If you give links to other blogs or websites, make sure you have visited them first and are certain of their content.

Talk to your reader. Most blogs are written in a slightly informal, conversational English. This is what readers expect. It gives them the feeling that they have formed a relationship with the writer and are connecting with them. Try to imagine that you are *chatting* to your reader. **Use the sort of words and phrases that you would naturally use in conversation** with a friend. This may include words and phrases that you would not use in other forms of writing.

Be yourself. People want to read blogs with original writing and original ideas. If they come back to your blog, it is because they like reading about what *you* have to say and they want to see how *you* say it. Be confident in your style and never try to write like someone else.

Do not be afraid to start your sentences with *I*. Generally, people do not expect blogs to read like newspapers. In other words, they do not visit a blog to read a report of facts. Most people read blogs because they give them a chance to learn about other people. They want to know *what the writer has done* and *how the writer feels* about things. **Tell your reader in the first person about your experiences and opinions**.

> **Tip for success**
> Once you have developed a style of writing that you are
> happy with, keep using that style.

Keep your blog short. Most people spend only a few minutes of their day or week reading blogs. They do not have time to read a lot, no matter how interesting or amusing the writing is. Do not fill the screen with text. Leave some white space and create a clean, simple screen that the reader knows they can deal with quickly.

Write a post that readers can scan. Remember that many people who visit a blog do not read the whole text word for word. Instead they *scan* the screen to get an idea of what the post is about or what information it might contain. They may want to get the general idea of what you have written or they may want only to find particular information. Present your blog in such a way that people scanning the text can get the most from it. You can do this by:

- writing in **short paragraphs**. It is much easier to scan a text that is broken up into many short *chunks* rather than one long block of text.

- providing **lists of information**, introduced by bullets. Lists are quick and easy to understand.

- providing a number of **relevant titles** to break up your text. Titles naturally attract the eye and can help guide the reader to a particular part of the post.

- highlighting important text in bold, color, or by formatting it as a hyperlink.

Communicate your message quickly. Whatever message or information you are trying to communicate in your post, make sure you do it within the first few lines. Do not assume that the reader has the time or the interest to read through a long introduction. Start your point immediately you start writing.

Make use of pictures. Select attractive and relevant images to break up blocks of text. Even if your images are only for decoration, they will still make the screen look more professional and more appealing.

Finally, when you have finished writing your post, **edit your writing**. The tone of your blog might be relaxed and informal but you still need the writing itself to be correct. Some readers will stop visiting a blog because it is poorly written even though they are interested in the topic. Take time to:

- remove phrases or words that are not needed
- change the order of paragraphs if this improves the post
- correct errors
- correct punctuation

Key point to remember
Get your reader's attention by saying what is most important within the first few lines.

Essays

Writing essays requires effort and a lot of people struggle with some aspect of it. However, it is a worthwhile skill to develop and practice. The ability to write an effective essay will help you in many other kinds of informational or persuasive writing. There are a number of things that you can do to make the task easier.

Give yourself enough time. In order to write the best essay possible you will probably need to read about the essay topic and research it. All of this takes time. Writing an essay hours before you have to hand it in is very stressful and rarely results in an excellent essay. Help yourself by starting your essay well before the deadline.

Learn from others. Read essays that other people have written on a range of subjects. Consider:

- How does the writer introduce the topic?
- What phrases do they use to present their points?
- How have they linked those points?
- Do they present their points in a logical order?
- Does the conclusion successfully bring together all the ideas and points presented in the essay?

Has the writer succeeded in any of the above and, if so, what can you learn from this?

Never plagiarize. If you use someone else's words, always give the name of the person who wrote or said those words and the title of the work in which the words appeared. Never pretend that someone else's words are your own. If you plagiarize you will cancel the good effect of any of your own work in an essay because your readers will not respect your ability or opinions.

If you have been given a specific essay title or topic, **read and then reread it**. Before you start even to plan your essay make absolutely sure that you **understand the title or topic** and what it is asking you to do. Remember that this is one of the main points on which your essay will be judged. This point may sound obvious, but failure to follow instructions is one of the commonest reasons for essays receiving a low grade.

As you write more essays, you will notice that certain verbs are used again and again in essay assignments. Here are some of the most common of these, together with their meanings. Make sure that you know exactly what each verb means in the context of an essay title:

- **analyze**: to examine something in detail for the purposes of explaining it
- **assess**: to judge how valuable, important, or successful something is
- **compare**: to look for similarities between
- **contrast**: to look for differences between
- **evaluate**: to judge how valuable, important, or successful something is
- **illustrate**: to explain something by using examples
- **outline**: to describe the most important points
- **relate**: to show how two or more issues are connected
- **summarize**: to describe the most important points

> **Key point to remember**
> No matter how well written your essay is, if you fail to address the subject of your essay properly, you will lose points.

Take time to **plan your essay**. Proper planning will help you to organize and develop your thoughts so that you are clear about what you want to write. It will also ensure that you do not leave anything out. Planning does not need to take a lot of time, and there are a number of helpful and imaginative ways that you can do it. There is a section on planning your work near the beginning of this book.

Keep to the point. Do not introduce unrelated subjects or aspects of a subject that are not relevant. Even if your points are interesting, you will not gain points for them! Ask yourself before you introduce a subject or make a point, how does this contribute to the essay assignment?

Make every word count. Write clearly and concisely, avoiding overlong sentences, meaningless phrases, and unnecessary adjectives. You will want to show that you have a varied vocabulary but do not be tempted to use a lot of words where a few well-chosen words will do!

Remember paragraphs. As a general rule, every time you make a separate point, start a new paragraph. Do not make your paragraphs too long. If a paragraph is very long, consider dividing it into separate points.

Remember that the type of English that is right for essays is a **slightly formal English**. It is more formal than the English that we usually use for speaking and writing emails. The English generally used in essays does not:

- include informal or slang words (unless you are quoting someone)
- include contractions, such as *isn't* and *won't*
- generally include phrases that use the words *I, me,* or *my*

Finally, when you have finished your essay, make sure you **read it carefully at least twice**. Be prepared at this point to make changes to it. Consider:

- the order of the points that you make. Is this logical and does your argument flow?
- your choice of language. Is it clear and does it say exactly what you intended it to say?

Look out too for:

- spelling errors
- typing mistakes (the informal name for this is typo)
- repetition of particular words. If you find you have used a word many times, consider replacing it with a synonym (a word with a similar meaning).

Tip for success

Use your computer's spellchecker to check your finished work but make sure that you read your essay for spelling errors too. You are more likely to find these if you read your essay aloud. Remember that a spellchecker will not find a typo such as "from" where the intended word is "form."

Essay phrases and words

There are **different stages to an essay** and each stage of the essay requires you to do different things. Under the relevant heading below, you will see a range of words and phrases that can be used at a particular stage or for a particular purpose. Use these words and phrases to express your ideas in a way that is more precise and more varied.

Introductions

The following notes will help you with many of the issues you need to cover in your introduction:

Introducing the topic and purpose of an essay
Here you **say briefly what you will discuss,** making sure that the title of your essay reflects this:

- *This essay will examine/look at ...*
- *This essay focuses on/discusses ...*
- *This essay considers/explores ...*
- *The aim of this essay is to assess/examine ...*
- *This essay seeks to evaluate/examine ...*

Defining key terms used in the essay
If there is any doubt about the meaning of a word or phrase that is important in your essay, **explain** in your introduction **what *you* mean** by that word or phrase:

- *Throughout this essay the term "x" will refer to ...*
- *The term "x" refers here to ...*
- *For the purposes of this essay, the term "x" is used to mean ...*

Explaining how the essay is organized
You may like to give a very **brief summary of the structure** of your essay. This shows the teacher/professor that you have arranged your

thoughts and arguments in an organized way. It will also make it easier for them to understand exactly what you are saying:

- *This essay is divided into three parts. The first part looks at ...*
- *There are three parts to this essay. The first part deals ...*
- *This essay has been structured in the following way.*
- *This essay begins by ... It then looks at ...*
- *The first part of this essay examines/looks at ...*

Saying why the topic is particularly interesting or important

You may like to **put the topic in context**, especially if the topic is of particular relevance now:

- *It is often said that ...*
- *We live in a world in which ...*
- *The issue of x is one that affects everyone ...*
- *Recent years have seen an increasing interest in ...*
- *The past decade has seen the rapid growth of ...*
- *One of the most important developments in recent years is ...*

Raising an area of your topic where there is disagreement or controversy

You might want to **offer arguments against** an idea suggested by your essay title, especially if you know of recent findings that seem to contradict it. If your essay title includes a question, it is always a good idea to do this.

- *This is not always true, however.*
- *This is not always the case, however.*
- *However, recent evidence suggests that this may not be the case.*
- *More recently, research has emerged that seems to contradict ...*
- *Concerns have been recently been raised about ...*
- *There is increasing concern about ...*
- *Not everyone agrees with this statement, however ...*
- *Not everyone is in favor of x, however ...*

Mentioning an area of your topic where there is a lack of knowledge
Again, this offers you the opportunity to introduce an argument against a statement or question in the essay title or to at least to **show that there is doubt** about the subject.

- *Less is known, however, about the effects of ...*
- *So far there has been little discussion of ...*
- *However, very little attention has been paid to ...*
- *We hear a lot about x but we hear less about y.*

The main part of the essay

This is the part of the essay where you **discuss and develop the ideas** that you outlined in your introduction. In this part of the essay, you will need to do several things. For example, you need to give facts and make statements; justify or disagree with statements; give reasons; and suggest causes. The following notes will help you with many of the issues you need to cover in the main part of your essay:

Stating what is generally considered to be true
You will probably want to **introduce a statement that everyone** – or most people – **agree is true**. (You might then develop the point or go on to argue against that point.)

- *It is often said that ...*
- *It is certainly true that ...*
- *It can be demonstrated that ...*
- *It is certainly the case that ...*
- *It is undoubtedly the case that ...*
- *No one would argue that ...*
- *Few people would argue that ...*
- *Few would argue that ...*

Stating that something is partly true
You may **only partly agree** with a statement:

- *There is an element of truth in this statement.*
- *There is some degree of truth in this.*
- *This is to some extent true.*
- *This is to some degree true.*

Key point to remember
When giving personal opinions in academic essays, it is generally better to avoid phrases that use the words *I*, *me*, or *my*:

✗ *I think that keeping animals in captivity is wrong for the following reasons:*
✗ *It's my opinion that keeping animals in captivity is wrong for the following reasons:*
✔ *Keeping animals in captivity is wrong for the following reasons:*

Providing facts
You might like to **refer to some new information** or statistics that relate to your topic:

- *Recent research clearly indicates/shows …*
- *Recent research suggests …*
- *A new study confirms that …*
- *A recent report revealed …*
- *It has recently emerged that …*

Useful words and phrases
The verbs *seem* and *appear* can be used to make these claims less definite, for example:

Government-funded research into this area appears to/seems to confirm this theory.

Suggesting reasons for something

You might want to **suggest an explanation** – or more than one explanation – for a situation or problem that you have described:

- *Perhaps this is because ...*
- *It might be that this is caused ...*
- *This may be because of/caused by ...*
- *This may be a result/consequence of ...*
- *It is likely/possible that ...*
- *We might assume from this that ...*
- *One possible explanation is that ...*
- *We might deduce from this that ...*

Describing the result of something

If you have stated the cause of something, you might want to **say what the result is**. These words can be used to start sentences that link the cause of something with the outcome.

- *Consequently ...*
- *As a result/consequence ...*
- *The result is ...*
- *The consequence is ...*
- *It follows that ...*
- *Therefore ...*

Adding to a point that you made before

You might like to **add to a previous point**, either by saying something that you think is **equally important**:

- *Besides, ...*
- *In addition, ...*
- *Similarly, ...*
- *In the same way, ...*

or by giving a point that is **even more important**:

- *What is more, ...*
- *Furthermore, ...*
- *Moreover, ...*
- *More importantly, ...*

Introducing examples

You will almost certainly want to **provide examples of what you are claiming**. Examples provide proof for your claim and can be introduced with the following words:

- *For example ...*
- *For instance ...*
- *A good example of this is ...*
- *This can be demonstrated by ...*
- *As evidence of this, ...*
- *An illustration/instance of this is ...*

> **Useful words and phrases**
> Alternatives to the phrase *good example* are *notable example* and *prime example*.

Note that you can vary the structure of your sentences by sometimes using the phrases *for example* and *for instance* in the middle of a sentence, with commas before and after:

- *Paper recycling, **for example**, is now common practice in most countries.*

- *Cycling to work, **for instance**, can significantly reduce your carbon footprint.*

You may want to highlight the importance of one particular example, in the following way:

- Environmental issues, ***particularly/in particular*** global warming, dominate the news.

- Environmental issues, **_notably/chiefly_** climate change and recycling, are at last being addressed.

Giving different opinions

Whatever your view on a subject, you will probably need to **show that you are aware of different views**, with phrases such as:

- *It could/might be argued that ...*
- *It is sometimes said that ...*
- *There are those who claim that ...*
- *Some claim that ...*
- *Another way of looking at/viewing this is ...*

Discussing differences

You may want to **highlight the differences** between two things:

- *There is a marked/sharp contrast between ...*
- *X is in sharp/stark contrast to y*
- *There is a clear distinction between x and y*
- *There are significant differences between x and y*
- *This contrasts sharply with ...*
- *X differs/varies widely*
- *By/In contrast, ...*
- *By/In comparison, ...*
- *Conversely, ...*

> #### Key point to remember
> Remember that the phrases *in contrast*, *by comparison*, and *conversely* can appear in the middle of a sentence, (with commas before and after), as well as at the start of a sentence, e.g.:
>
> *Carlos was clever, handsome, and charismatic. His brother, in contrast, was a plain, shy man.*
> *Carlos was clever, handsome, and charismatic. In contrast, his brother was a plain, shy man.*

Reporting what someone else has said

You will sometimes want to **quote what someone else has said or written**. There are many reasons for doing this. You might want to provide support for own opinion or you may want to introduce an opinion that you can then disagree with.

- Smith asserts/claims/proposes/suggests that ...
- Smith maintains/states that ...
- Jones comments/observes//remarks/reports/writes that ...
- Jones concludes that ...
- According to Jones, ...
- As Jones states/points out, ...
- In Jones's view/opinion, ...
- Jones's view/opinion is that ...

> **Key point to remember**
> Note that the present tense is usually used in such phrases.

Introducing quotations

Often, you will need to **name not only the author of a quotation, but also the text** that the quotation comes from. This can be done in a number of ways, so it is a good idea to ask your teacher if there is a recommended style:

- Blake (1998, p. 62) asserts that "Walker hated his mother."
- Blake[1] claims that "Walker hated his mother."
- As Blake (1998, p. 62) points out, Walker had a difficult relationship with his mother.
- Blake (1998, p. 62) maintains that Walker had a difficult relationship with his mother.

Saying the same thing in a different way

You will sometimes want to **make clear exactly what it is that you are saying** by repeating your point in a way that is briefer and simpler.

- *In other words, ...*
- *To put it simply, ...*
- *To put it more simply, ...*
- *That is to say, ...*
- *To look at this another way, ...*

Conclusions

The conclusion brings together all the ideas and information you have discussed. It shows the reader that the essay is complete and that the aims of the essay have been achieved. In a conclusion, you **summarize the main points** and say what the consequences of your evidence are:

- *In summary, ...*
- *To summarize, ...*
- *To sum up briefly, ...*
- *In conclusion, ...*
- *To conclude, ...*
- *It can be concluded that ...*
- *We can therefore conclude that ...*

Papers, theses, and dissertations

A paper is a piece of writing on a particular subject that is usually longer than an essay, especially one that a student does as a requirement for course work. A thesis (plural *theses*) is a longer paper based on a student's personal research that is submitted as an important requirement for a college or university degree (usually a bachelor's or master's degree). A dissertation is an even longer paper, based on original research, that is typically written as the main requirement for a doctoral degree (Ph.D.). Theses and dissertations are usually divided into a series of numbered chapters.

All of these texts are like an essay in that they are **formal in style**. The type of language that is suitable for essays is suitable for these kinds of papers. They do not:

- include informal or slang words
- include contractions, such as *isn't* and *won't*
- generally include phrases that use the words *I*, *me*, or *my*

For help with formal writing, especially phrases and words to use in these longer texts, see the part in this book on writing essays.

If you are assigned a paper to write or you have to write one as part of a degree requirement, you will probably be given a target length. Both a thesis and a dissertation are **very much longer than a normal paper**. They can be anything up to 10,000 words long and some dissertations are as long as books – in fact many are published as books if there is sufficient interest in them.

Theses and dissertations have a **more complicated structure** than an essay or a shorter paper. This is partly because they are so much longer and partly because they examine their subjects in greater depth. It is important to note that the *exact* structure of a thesis or dissertation will vary depending on:

- the area of study of the dissertation. Different subjects require different structures.
- the school you attend, or the department within that school. Different colleges and universities have different rules on how to structure a dissertation.

> **Key point to remember**
> Before you even start to plan your thesis or dissertation, make sure you have a copy of your department's rules on how to structure it.

As we have said, the structure of a thesis or dissertation will vary, depending on the university and the subject. It is your responsibility to make sure you know exactly what your university or subject requires. The general features of the structure that are given here are therefore only a rough guide:

Title Page
Among other details, this page will include:

- the title of the work
- the name of the writer
- the qualification for which the dissertation has been written
- the relevant university or other place of study
- the date that the dissertation was submitted

Table of contents
This is an index of everything that is contained in the paper except the title page and the table of contents itself.

Abstract
This will say in general terms what the dissertation is about. An appropriate length is generally agreed to be about 300-500 words.

Main part of the work

This will be divided into sections or chapters. The sections or chapters will each have an introduction, a main part and a conclusion. However, it is very important that there is a link between these subsections. When you are writing this part of your work, try to remember that the reader must at all times understand how one part relates to another.

Conclusion

This is where you help the reader to understand the significance of your conclusions, rather than just restating your conclusions. It can be a challenging part of your paper to write. Some people find it helpful to write this part a little time after the main body of the text. This allows them to think more clearly about everything that they have written and to make judgments about it.

Bibliography

This should be a complete list of the books, articles, and other references that you have used in your paper.

> **Tip for success**
> Do not delay preparing your bibliography until the end of your work. Prepare it as you are writing, keeping track of the books and other sources that you use.

Theses and dissertations are complicated pieces of work and are not easy to write. You can help yourself with this challenging task by **planning the structure of your work very thoroughly**. You will want to show the plan to your supervisor before you start to write it. Your discussions with your supervisor will very often result in changes to your plan so **allow yourself plenty of time for the planning stage** of the process.

For general help with planning a piece of writing, see the section on planning near the beginning of this book.

When you are ready to start writing, **do not assume that you must start at the first chapter and finish with the last**. Many people find that there is an area of the work that they are more confident about. Consider starting with that area of the subject.

Most colleges and universities have a set of rules about how to present advanced papers. These rules concern, for example, the type and size of font used, the type of paper written on and the layout of the page. **Make sure that you have a copy of the presentation guidelines for your university and that you follow them.**

The **rules for good writing apply to papers, theses, and dissertations** as they do to any other form of written work. For general help with formal writing, see the chapters in this book on writing essays and writing reports. It is worth repeating some of these rules here as they are especially true of long, complicated pieces of writing.

Write clearly. You know what you mean by your writing but if you do not express yourself clearly your reader may not. Make sure your reader does not have to struggle to understand your English.

Write concisely, avoiding overlong sentences and unnecessary adjectives. These will make your English difficult to follow.

Avoid repetition. If you find you have used a word many times, consider replacing it with a synonym (a word with a similar meaning).

Remember paragraphs. Text should never appear as a long block. As general rule, every time you make a separate point, start a new paragraph.

Write paragraphs of the right length. They should not be too long or too short. Never write a paragraph of only one sentence.

> **Tip for success**
> Remember your reader at all times. Try to write English that is a pleasure to read.

You will almost certainly want to **write more than one draft of your work**. Rewriting is an extremely valuable part of the process. It can be hard to see where the problems are while you are writing a piece of text. It is only when you come back to the text that you see where changes need to be made. You may find at this stage that you need to:

- explain a point more clearly
- remove a point that is not relevant
- change the order of the points that you are making

The above changes all relate to the content of your work. As well as examining the content of your work, you will also need to **check it thoroughly for errors**.

Remember that a supervisor who has read parts of your work will only have commented on its content or structure. They will not have brought to your attention spelling or grammatical errors. Use your computer's spellchecker to check your finished work but make sure that you **read your work for spelling errors too**. Remember that a spellchecker will not find a typo such as *from* where the intended word is *form*.

> **Tip for success**
> Read your work through once simply in order to check for grammatical errors and spelling errors.

Reports

A report is a **written document that presents information about a particular subject** to a particular reader or group of readers. The writer of the report has usually been asked by the reader to prepare the report.

Reports are written by people who work in many areas, for example, business, government and education. Many jobs will require you to write a report at some time, even if writing is not a usual part of the job. This is one reason that it is important to develop competent writing skills, no matter what your line of work.

All **reports present a number of facts** that the writer examines in detail. The writer then makes judgments based on those facts. Many reports also make recommendations about things that should be done because of the facts that they have described.

Before you start writing a report, make sure that you **know exactly what it is that you want to achieve**. It may help you to form a clearer idea if you write a short paragraph describing the purpose of it.

Make sure too that you **know exactly who you are writing the report for**. You may be writing for readers with the same understanding of the subject and the same interests, or you may be writing for different types of reader. Your report will need to cover everything that your readers are expecting.

Like an essay, a report is a **formal piece of writing**. The type of English that is right for reports does not:

• include informal or slang words

• include contractions, such as *isn't* and *won't*

• include words that imply a moral judgment, such as *horrible* and *atrocious*

- generally include phrases that include the words *I*, *me*, or *my*. (However, note that if the report includes recommendations, this part of the report may use such phrases.)

Although the English in your report should be formal, it should also be **clear and *readable***. "Formal" is not the same as "difficult." You want your reader **to understand quickly** what you have written without having to make a lot of effort. Although it may not be possible to write a report that your reader actively enjoys reading, you do not want the reader to struggle to get through it!

Do not use long, difficult words in order to impress the reader. The use of a lot of hard words can have the effect of making your writing less readable. Most readers prefer plainer, more direct English. For example, if you find yourself writing the verb *utilize*, consider whether the simpler verb *use* could be used instead. Likewise, if you write *dwelling*, ask yourself whether *home* would in fact be better.

Do not write long sentences. Of course you will want to write some longer and some shorter sentences in order to provide some variety in your English. However, you should try to avoid very long, complicated sentences as they are difficult to understand. Look at the following sentence:

> In terms of numbers, this is essentially an increase, albeit a small increase, and we look forward to seeing this trend continue over the forthcoming weeks and months.

Now see how a shorter sentence can say the same thing much more clearly:

> This is an increase, albeit a small one, and we look forward to seeing this trend continue.

Notice in the first sentence, the phrases and words:

- in terms of
- essentially
- over the forthcoming weeks and months

These words and phrases have little or no meaning in this sentence. In the second sentence, the writer has removed them without changing the meaning. If you have written a long sentence, examine the various parts of that sentence and consider whether any of the words are not needed.

As we have said, the main purpose of a report is to present facts about a subject. The purpose is *not* to describe the writer's opinions or feelings on the subject. For this reason, **do not use the words** *I*, *me*, **or** *my* **in your writing.** You may need to suggest ideas and give possible explanations for certain facts, but you should not do so with phrases such as "it seems to me" and "in my opinion." Compare the sentences below:

> ✗ *The same quarter saw sales in these markets rise by 13 percent, a development that I am convinced is due to better marketing of these products.*

> ✔ *The same quarter saw sales in these markets rise by 13 percent, almost certainly as a result of better marketing of these products.*

Similarly, the language that you use in your report:

- should not show your feelings
- should make appeals to strong feelings in your readers

For this reason, avoid words such as *appalling*, *terrible*, and *fantastic*. Instead use adjectives that express the same idea but in a calmer, more formal way, without suggesting an emotional reaction. Compare these sentences:

✗ *Sales for the last quarter of the year were terrible.*
✓ *Sales for the last quarter of the year were very disappointing.*

✗ *This was a fantastic achievement.*
✓ *This was a remarkable achievement.*

Remember that some people will not want to read the whole report, word for word. Instead they will want to *scan* it, getting the general idea of what you have written or looking for particular information. Present your report in a way that **allows people to read it quickly**. Consider:

- writing in **short paragraphs**. It is much easier to scan a text that is made of many short *chunks* rather than one long block of text.

- giving information in the form of **bullets**. Bulleted lists are quick to understand and are an acceptable way of presenting information in reports.

- breaking up your text with **headings**. Headings will guide the reader to the parts of the report that they are interested in.

The main purpose of a report is to present information. Unlike an essay, a report need not always present information in the form of written paragraphs. You can show information very effectively in the form of **bulleted lists, tables, diagrams and charts**. Label any tables and diagrams, etc., clearly. Information shown in this way should relate to the writing in your report, for example:

Figure 1 shows that overall sales increased by 3% in the third quarter.
Overall sales increased by 3% in the third quarter (see Figure 1).

The structure of a report

The **structure of your report** will partly depend on what is contained in it. However, most reports have a fairly similar structure:

1 Title page
2 Contents list
3 Executive summary or abstract
4 Introduction
5 Main part of the report
6 Conclusions
7 Recommendations
8 Appendices
9 Bibliography

1 Title Page
Include the following formation in your title page:

- The title of the report.
- The purpose of the report.
- Your name and the name of the person or group that you have written the report for.
- The date that you sent or gave the report to the reader(s).

2 Contents list
If you have written a long report, you will need to provide a contents list. This gives the main sections and chapters of the report and the pages on which the reader will find those sections and chapters. If your report contains many charts, tables, or illustrations, it is helpful to provide separate lists for these at the beginning of the report.

3 Executive summary or abstract
You need to give a **summary of the report** – often called an executive summary rather than an abstract when you are writing a report. Here you describe briefly the most important information that is in the report. The summary should not be long – no more than ten percent of the total report. As a rough guide, write one sentence for every main

section of your report. It is helpful to summarize your conclusions in this part of a report for readers who will read only the summary, and not the whole report.

4 Introduction
Here, you should give the following information:

- Any background information relating to the subject that the reader should be aware of.
- The purpose of the report.
- Exactly which areas of your subject you deal with in the report.

5 Body of the report
This is the longest part of the report, where you say:

- what you discovered when you examined this subject
- what you decided was true after considering all the facts (the conclusions)

You will probably need to divide this part of the report into sections. Each paragraph or group of paragraphs on the same subject is a section. It is likely that each section will also need dividing into subsections. These sections and subsections will need to be numbered. The system used by most report writers is as follows:

- Each section in the main part of the report is numbered 1,2,3, etc.
- Sections within those main sections (subsections) are then numbered 1.1, 1.2, 1.3, 1.4, etc.
- If there are any subsections of those subsections, they appear as 1.1.1, 1.1.2, etc.

6 Conclusions
This is the stage at which you bring together all the conclusions that you reached in the main part of your report. Present these conclusions in the order in which they appeared. **Do not include any new information** here.

7 Recommendations

Some reports do not include recommendations. They present and examine facts but do not make suggestions about what should be done because of those facts. Some reports do include recommendations and set them out here, in a separate part of the report. Note that some reports include recommendations in the conclusion or even in the executive summary.

8 Appendices

This is the place to put information which is referred to in the report but is too detailed or complicated to include in the main part of the report. The sort of information you would put here includes:

* questionnaires
* long, detailed tables or other small points of information that most people would think it a chore to read
* any instructions for research referred to in the report
* a glossary (that is, a list of technical terms with their definitions that are used in the report)

9 Bibliography

If you refer to other people's work in your report, give the following information here:

* the author's or authors' name(s)
* the work's full title
* the name of the publisher and place where it was published
* the year it was first published or, the number of the edition and the date it was published

Finally, when you have finished writing your report, **read it carefully from beginning to end**. Be prepared at this point to make changes to it. Consider:

* the order in which you have given the facts. Is it logical?

- the conclusions that you have reached. Are they reasonable, considering the evidence that you have given?

- your choice of language. Is it clear and does it say exactly what you intended it to say?

If possible, leave your corrected report and come back to it a day later. Are you still satisfied with every part of it? Is there any part that you now feel you need to change? **Many people write several drafts of a report** before they are happy with it.

While you are rereading your report, look out too for:

- typos and spelling errors

- repetition of particular words. If you find you have used a word many times, consider replacing it with a synonym (a word with a similar meaning).

- Unnecessary words. Look out for words which mean nothing. For example, a word such as *basically* may have no meaning in a sentence.

Report phrases and words

There are **different stages to a report** and each stage of the report requires you to do different things. Under the relevant headings below, you will see a range of words and phrases that can be used at a particular stage or for a particular purpose. Use these words and phrases to express your ideas in a way that is more precise and more varied.

Introductions

Introducing the topic and purpose of the report

Here you **explain the purpose of your report** and say exactly which areas of the subject your report deals with:

- *This report will examine/look at ...*
- *This report aims to/sets out to examine ...*
- *This report focuses on ...*
- *This report considers/explores ...*
- *The aim/purpose of this report is to assess/examine ...*
- *This report seeks to evaluate/examine ...*
- *This report begins by ... It then looks at ...*
- *The first part of this report examines/looks at ...*

Defining key terms used in the report

If there is any doubt about the meaning of a word or phrase that is important in your report, **explain** in your introduction **what you mean** by that word or phrase:

- *Throughout this report the term 'x' will refer to ...*
- *The term 'x' refers here to ...*
- *For the purposes of this report, the term 'x' is used to mean ...*

If your report has many technical terms that will need explaining to some readers, consider putting them in a glossary within your appendix (see above).

Raising an area of the subject where there is disagreement or controversy

You might like to **offer arguments against** something that people generally think is true.

- *This is not always true, however.*
- *This is not always the case, however.*
- *However, recent evidence suggests that this may not be the case.*
- *More recently, research has emerged that seems to contradict ...*
- *Concerns have been recently been raised about ...*
- *There is increasing concern about ...*
- *Not everyone agrees with this statement, however ...*
- *Not everyone is in favor of x, however ...*

Mentioning an area of the subject where there is a lack of knowledge

You might want to **raise an area of your report's subject that little is known about**:

- *Less is known, however, about the effects of ...*
- *So far there has been little discussion of ...*
- *However, very little attention has been paid to ...*
- *We hear a lot about x but we hear less about y.*

Referring to new information

You might like to **refer to some new information or statistics** that relate to the subject of the report:

- *Recent research clearly indicates/shows ...*
- *Recent research suggests ...*
- *Recent findings suggest ...*
- *A new study confirms that ...*
- *A recent report revealed ...*
- *It has recently emerged that ...*

> **Useful words and phrases**
> The verbs *seem* and *appear* can be used to make these claims less definite, for example:
>
> *These recent findings appear to/seem to confirm this theory.*

Main part of the report

This is where you describe exactly what you discovered when you examined the report's subject:

Suggesting reasons for something
You might want to **suggest an explanation** – or more than one explanation – for a situation or problem that you have described:

- *Perhaps this is because ...*
- *It might be that this is caused ...*
- *This may be because of/caused by ...*
- *This may be a result/consequence of ...*
- *It is likely/possible that ...*
- *We might assume from this that ...*
- *One possible explanation is that ...*
- *We might deduce from this that ...*

Describing the result of something
If you have stated the cause of something, you might want to **say what the result is**. These words can be used to start sentences that link the cause of something with the outcome:

- *Consequently ...*
- *As a result/consequence ...*
- *The result is ...*
- *The consequence is ...*
- *It follows that ...*
- *Therefore ...*

Adding to a point that you made before
You might like to **add to a previous point**, either by saying something that you think is **equally important**:

- *Besides, ...*
- *In addition, ...*
- *Similarly, ...*
- *In the same way, ...*

or by giving a point that is **even more important**:

- *What is more, ...*
- *Furthermore, ...*
- *Moreover, ...*
- *More importantly, ...*

Discussing differences
You may want to **highlight the differences** between two things

- *There is a marked/sharp contrast between ...*
- *There is a clear distinction between x and y*
- *There are significant differences between x and y*
- *This contrasts sharply with ...*
- *X differs/varies widely*
- *By/In contrast, ...*
- *By/In comparison, ...*
- *Conversely, ...*

> **Key point to remember**
> Remember that the phrases *in contrast, by comparison*
> and *conversely* can appear in the middle of a sentence,
> (with commas before and after), as well as at the start
> of a sentence, e.g.:
> *Group A suffered few colds and infections. Group B, in contrast,
> reported constant ill-health.*
> *Group A suffered few colds and infections. In contrast, Group B
> reported constant ill-health.*

Reporting what someone else has said

You will sometimes want to **quote what someone else has said or
written**:

- *Smith asserts/claims/proposes/suggests that ...*
- *Smith maintains/states that ...*
- *Jones comments/observes//remarks/reports/writes that ...*
- *Jones concludes that ...*
- *According to Jones, ...*
- *As Jones states/points out, ...*
- *In Jones's view/opinion, ...*
- *Jones's view/opinion is that ...*

> **Key point to remember**
> Note that the present tense is usually used in such phrases.

Introducing quotations

Often, you will need to **name not only the author of a quotation, but
also the piece of writing** that the quotation comes from. This can be
done in a number of ways:

- *Blake (1998, p. 62) asserts that "Rogers was at fault here."*
- *Blake1 claims that "Rogers was at fault here."*
- *As Blake (1998, p. 62) points out, Rogers was at fault here.*
- *Blake (1998, p. 62) maintains that Rogers was at fault here.*

Conclusions

Summarizing

You will want to **summarize the main points of your report**:

- *In summary, ...*
- *To summarize, ...*
- *In conclusion, ...*
- *To conclude, ...*
- *It can be concluded that ...*
- *We can therefore conclude that ...*
- *The following points summarize our key findings:*
- *The key findings are outlined below:*
- *It is clear that ...*
- *No conclusions were reached regarding ...*

Recommending

You may want to **advise the reader that something should be done**:

- *We strongly recommend that ...*
- *It is my recommendation that ...*
- *It is essential that ...*
- *It would be advisable to ...*
- *I urge x to ...*

Presentations

A presentation is a speech in which you provide information to an audience about a subject that you have researched, written about, or that you know more about than they do. Most presentations are accompanied by visual aids such as slides.

Why write a presentation?

The process of writing your presentation will help you to **decide** the **key points** of your material so that you know exactly what you want to say. Deciding what to include – and what *not* to include – is very important and the key to a successful presentation.

As you write your presentation, you will think of the most **logical order** in which to present your main points.

You will also make sensible decisions about what **slides**, **objects**, or other **visual aids** you need for your talk.

By writing the whole of your presentation in advance, you can make sure that your talk is the **right length**. It is no use preparing a brilliant talk that you cannot possibly give in the time allowed. On the other hand, you do not want to finish your talk 20 minutes early!

Giving presentations can be stressful and many people feel anxious about talking to large groups of people. If you know that you have **prepared your presentation properly**, it will give you confidence on the day.

> **Key point to remember**
> Don't leave it to the last minute to prepare your presentation. Have your presentation finished at least 24 hours in advance.

Deciding the content

Whatever your presentation is about, before you start writing it, ask yourself the following question: **What am I trying to achieve with this talk?**

The best way to be clear about this is to ask two questions:

1 **Who** is this presentation for?
2 **What** is my key message?

Who?
Always write a presentation that is suitable for your audience. Try to find out in advance as much as possible about the audience and what they will **expect from you**. If possible, speak to someone else who has given a presentation to the same audience, or at least speak to the person who has organized the talk. It will help you to plan your talk if you know the following about your audience:

• how much knowledge of your subject they have
• their level of education
• how old they are
• how long they are able or willing to listen to a speaker

What?
The **key message** is the main thing that you want your audience to learn from your presentation – or very often, the main two or three things. Before you even start to write your talk, decide what your key message is.

While you are thinking of the **purpose of the presentation**, consider these questions. Is the purpose:

- to **give your audience information**?
- to **persuade your audience to do something, for example to buy something**?
- to **entertain**?
- to **allow the audience to get to know you**?

Most presentations are intended to give the audience information. If this is your main purpose, make sure you **give the right amount of information**: too much and your audience will be unable to take it in; too little and your audience may feel that they have wasted their time.

It may not be appropriate to entertain your audience – this will, of course, depend on the subject that you are speaking about. However, when you are planning your talk, keep in mind that most people find it hard to concentrate when a speaker makes no attempt to keep their interest.

> **Key point to remember**
> Remember that if you entertain your audience, you will
> be more likely to persuade them or inform them!

When planning a presentation, it is useful to break it down into three parts: **the beginning, the middle, and the end**.

In the beginning part of your presentation, try to get your audience's attention. You might ask them to do a short activity or perhaps ask them a question. Choose something that will wake them up and involve them. **Make your audience listen to you!**

In the middle part of the presentation, **tell them the facts** that they need to know. Keep it simple and limit yourself to what is really important. Do not tell your audience more than they can understand and remember.

Be aware that the last part of your presentation is possibly the most important part. The audience are more likely to remember what you tell them at the end of your presentation than in the middle. Whatever your **key message** is, make sure that you **say it – or repeat it – at the end**.

> **Key points to remember**
> Involve your audience.
> Repeat your key message in the last part of your presentation.

Writing notes for a presentation

Make good notes to help you give your presentation. Very few people can give a full presentation without looking at their notes now and then. Audiences do not expect speakers to be able to do this. Write only the **main points** of your talk on **numbered index cards or prompt cards**. Write one or two key points on each card and make the writing bigger and clearer than your usual handwriting. There are several good things about prompt cards:

- They remind or "prompt" you to say your next point but you do not read from them. Audiences like you to **look at them** and **speak to them**. A speaker who looks down and reads notes will not keep the audience's attention.

- They allow you to **see your next point very clearly**. (When you have finished saying one point, put the card to the bottom of the pile and you will see your next point.)

- They are **small**. The audience will not notice them, even if you look at them several times.

- You can **write the time** that you should get to each point **on each card**. This way you can make sure that you say everything you want to say in the time that is allowed.

Alternatively, rather than using prompt cards, you may want to use your slides as prompts for what you are going to talk about. These are described in the next section.

> **Tip for success**
> If you use prompt cards, number them and write the
> time that you should get to each point on the cards.

Writing slides for a presentation

Always **prepare your own slides**. Do not be tempted to use someone else's slides. There are several reasons for this:

- The process of preparing your own slides will help you to decide on your key points.

- It will also help you to present those points in a logical order.

- If you know exactly what is on each slide you will able to talk about each slide with confidence and authority.

Keep the **text** on your slides **simple and brief**. Do not put too much information on a slide (a very common mistake). Remember that although *you* will know your slides very well, *your audience* is looking at them for the first time. Make sure they can make sense of them very quickly. Remember too that they will only have a short time to understand what they are looking at. Limit the amount of text on a slide to **six or seven words on each line** and to **six or seven lines of text** per slide. The slide below, for example, gives as bulleted points the advantages of a new product, in this case a cleaning fluid:

Keener Cleaner

- effective
- economical
- good for the environment
- pleasant-smelling
- pleasant color
- recyclable bottle

It is important also to write the text of your slides **big enough to be seen**. Remember that if you are speaking to a lot of people in a large room, the people sitting at the back will need to be able to read your slides too.

It is a good idea to write a short **title** on each slide. This should be a single word or a short phrase. The purpose is to let your audience see immediately the subject of the slide. Make sure that your **titles** are **large** – larger than the rest of the text.

Edit your slides carefully. Look over them several times, checking the spelling and the phrasing. It is embarrassing to be told by a member of the audience that there is an error on one of your slides!

> **Tip for success**
> Limit the amount of text on a slide to **six or seven words on each line** and to **six or seven lines of text** per slide.

Presentation phrases

There are **different stages to a presentation** and each stage of the presentation requires you to do different things. Under the relevant heading below, you will see a range of words and phrases that can be used at a particular stage or for a particular purpose. Use these words and phrases to express your ideas in a way that is more precise and more varied.

Introducing yourself (and thanking your audience)

If you are new to presentations, it is a good idea to **write your introduction out in full on a prompt card**. Of course, you know this information yourself, but you may be very nervous at the start of your talk. It is easy to forget what you are saying when you are nervous. A written reminder of your first few lines will give you confidence:

- *Thank you very much for coming here today.*
- *First of all, I'd like to thank you all for coming here today.*
- *I'd like to start by thanking X, who invited me here to give this talk today.*
- *My name is Paola Sanchez and I'm the marketing manager for Now Systems.*
- *My name is Paola Sanchez and I'm here today to talk to you about ...*
- *Let me introduce myself. My name is Paola Sanchez and ...*

Introducing your talk

It is a good idea at the start of a presentation to tell your audience in a few words **what you are going to talk about**. If your audience have a clear understanding of what you are talking about from the start, it will help them to understand the whole of the talk:

- *Today/This afternoon I'm going to be talking about ...*
- *My subject today is ...*
- *The topic of my talk is ...*
- *I'm here today to tell you about ...*
- *My aim this afternoon is to ...*

You might then **tell your audience about the structure of your talk**. Again, this will help with their understanding:

* *First, we're going to take a look at ...*
* *After that, we'll be considering...*
* *Finally, we'll be thinking about ...*
* *I'm going to divide this talk into four parts. The first part deals with ... The second part looks at ... etc.*

> **Useful words and phrases**
> Notice that a speaker will often say "**We're** going to consider/look at," etc. This makes the audience feel involved in what the speaker is saying.

"Reminding" people

You will be stating facts in your presentation. Your **audience may already know** some of those facts. It is a good idea to show that you are aware of this:

* *As you know...*
* *You may be aware that ...*
* *You may have heard of ...*
* *I'm sure many of you will already know ...*
* *It's often said ...*

Referring to slides and other visual aids

It is likely that you will use slides or other visual aids as a part of a presentation. Try to **make a clear link between the slide and what you are saying**. The following phrases will help with this.

* *If you could just take a look at this slide ...*
* *This slide shows you ...*
* *This slide represents ...*
* *As you can see from this graph ...*
* *Looking at these figures, we can see that ...*

Giving more details
Often, in a presentation you make one point and then want to **give
further details about that particular point**:

- *I'd like to say a little more about this point …*
- *I'd like to add at this point that …*
- *Another relevant point here is …*
- *While we're on the subject of x, it's worth also saying …*
- *Let's consider/look at this in more detail…*
- *I'd like us to think about this for a moment …*

Changing the subject
At various points in your presentation, you will want to make a new
point. **Introduce each new point clearly**:

- *I'd like to move on now to the issue of …*
- *Moving on now to the subject of …*
- *Turning to the issue of…*
- *Let's turn now to the subject of …*
- *The next thing I'd like to think about/focus on is …*
- *Now we'll move on to the subject of …*
- *Let's look now at the question of …*

Using questions to make a point
You can **introduce a point by asking a question**. This might be a
general point or a point that will especially interest the audience:

- *So, how does this relate to us?*
- *So why is this of interest?*
- *So why have I brought this to your attention?*
- *So why is this an advantage/a benefit?*
- *How much will all of this cost?*
- *What does this mean for …?*
- *And why is this important/significant?*
- *So where does this lead/take us?*

> **Key point to remember:**
> Introduce each new point that you make clearly.

Paraphrasing (saying something in a different way)
You may want to make a point clear by **expressing something in a different way**. These phrases will help:

- *In other words ...*
- *So what I'm saying is....*
- *To put it another way ...*
- *To put it more simply ...*
- *Another way of putting this is ...*

Returning to a point you made earlier
You might want to **show how a new point relates to an earlier point** in the presentation:

- *As I said before ...*
- *Going back to what I said earlier ...*
- *To return to a point I made earlier ...*
- *Earlier in the talk, I mentioned ...*
- *You'll recall I mentioned x earlier ...*
- *This relates to a point I made earlier about ...*
- *Let's look back at something I said earlier ...*

> **Tip for success:**
> Linking a new point with something you said earlier will help your audience to understand your presentation.

Summarizing your presentation
Towards the end of your talk, you may like to **remind your audience of the main points** you have made:

- *We've covered a lot of ground today. Let me quickly summarize the main points ...*

- *Let's summarize briefly what we've looked at today …*
- *I'd like to quickly go over the main points of today's presentation …*
- *If I can just sum up the main points of the presentation …*
- *To finish, I'd just like to remind you of some of the issues we've covered today …*

Concluding

Now is the time to **tell your audience the thing – or the things – that you want them to remember**:

- *I'll conclude very briefly by saying that …*
- *I'll finish by saying …*
- *Let me end by …*
- *I'd like to leave you with this thought …*

Finishing a presentation

Most speakers like to **let their audience know that they have finished their presentation**:

- *I think that's everything I wanted to say today.*
- *I think I've covered everything I wanted to say today.*
- *I think that's about it.*

You will then want to **thank your audience** and, if there is time, **invite them to ask you questions** relating to the subject:

- *Thank you all very much for taking the time to listen to this presentation.*
- *Does anyone have any questions (or comments)?*
- *Would anyone like to ask any questions?*
- *Please feel free to ask questions.*
- *If anyone has any questions, I'd be very happy to answer them.*
- *We have ten minutes left now if anyone has any questions they would like to ask.*

> **Tip for success**
> Always let your audience know that you have finished your presentation and remember to thank them for listening.

Your work qualifications

When you apply for a job it is customary to submit a standard document that gives details of your work experience, education, and background. It also gives your full name and contact details. For most jobs, this document is called a résumé in American English. The word is properly written with accents but you will often see it without accents, as *resume*, because the context makes it clear that this is not the verb *resume*. In British English this document is called a CV (short for Latin *curriculum vitae*). The term CV and the short form *vitae* are also used in American English, but usually only for certain professions such as academia and medicine. In American usage, a CV is much more detailed, longer, and presented in a different format than a résumé.

People usually send a cover letter with their résumé or CV. You will find help with this type of letter in the part of this book on writing letters.

A résumé should be as short as possible without leaving out essential information. Job advertisements sometimes specify the maximum length of résumé that is acceptable, but in any case your résumé should rarely be longer than three pages, and if you can get everything important on one or two pages that is best.

Whether you are writing a one-page document or a two- to three-page document, there are a number of things that you must keep in mind. The first of these is that the reader of your résumé or CV will probably assess it along with *many* others. They will probably have limited time to do this. Therefore, your information must be:

- quick and easy to read
- clear and concise
- pleasant to look at

> **Key point to remember**
> Keep your résumé concise. The reader will not have time
> to read through five or six pages, no matter how
> impressive the details.

Remember that if your information is poorly presented, the reader will
be more likely to reject it even if your skills and experience make you
the perfect candidate for the job. Your résumé must therefore have:

- a **clear structure**. Be sure to organize the information under
  headings such as *education* and *experience*.

- **plenty of white space**. A dense page with too much text is difficult
  and unpleasant to read.

Make sure too that you print your résumé or CV on **good quality,
clean paper**. Remember that the reader does not know you. The only
evidence that they have of your character and your suitability for the
job is the paper they have in their hand. Make it look impressive. You
should also have an electronic version of your résumé that looks
equally impressive, and does not look simply like a paper version of
your information put on the screen. Many companies today do not
even accept paper résumés and prefer to receive information in
electronic format so that they can evaluate it computationally.

Remember that the information you include must be **relevant** to the
work. Do not be tempted to include facts that do not directly relate to
the job that you are applying for. A reader with little time to assess
several résumés might be distracted by this and may not actually see
the important information.

> **Key point to remember**
> Presentation is extremely important in résumé and CV
> writing. Two documents with the same information will be
> judged differently by the reader if one of them is more
> attractively presented and better organized than the other.

Here is a general layout for a résumé. The structure and layout of résumés varies but this format is generally accepted. Notice the clear headings and the white space around the paragraphs. If you need to write a résumé, look at one by someone who is in the same profession as you in order to learn how your information should be presented.

[1] **Mark Ortega** [2] 382 Danvers Court, Indianapolis, IN 46219
(317) 923-7102 [3] markort@lycos.com

[4] **Objective** A senior sales management position with a Fortune 500 company in the Midwestern or Mid-Atlantic states

[5] **Experience** 2006–2010 Trellis Components, Louisville, KY
National Sales Manager
- Increased sales from $50 million to $100 million.
- Doubled sales per representative from $5 million to $10 million.
- Suggested new products that increased earnings by 23%.

2003–2006 Massey and Barrett Castings Bowling Green, KY
District Sales Manager
- Increased regional sales from $25 million to $350 million.
- Managed 250 sales representatives in 10 Midwestern states.
- Implemented training course for new recruits – speeding profitability.

1997–2003 Doublair Ventilation Systems Nashville, TN
Senior Sales Representative
- Expanded sales team from 50 to 100 representatives.
- Tripled division revenues for each sales associate.
- Expanded sales to include mass market accounts.

1994–1997 DuraWare, Inc. Nashville, TN
Sales Representative
- Expanded territorial sales by 400%.
- Received company's highest sales award four years in a row.
- Developed Excellence In Sales training course.

[6] **Expertise** HVAC architecture
CAD design specification
JIT inventory management systems

[7] **Education** 1995–1997 Phoenix University Online MBA
1991–1995 Vanderbilt University BA

[8] **Interests** digital photography, NASCAR, soccer, genealogy

1. Give your name in full at the top of the résumé where it can easily be seen.
2. Also provide your contact details prominently at the top.
3. Always provide your email address.
4. Write your objective at the top of your résumé. Summarize what you want your next job to be.
5. Always provide details of your most recent employment first and then work backwards.
6. If you can summarize skills that will be of interest to potential employers it is a good idea to isolate these for easy reading. This is especially true for any software and other technical skills you possess.
7. Your education background should also be listed with the most recent/highest accomplishments first.
8. It is not essential to list your personal interests but for candidates who are otherwise equal, some personal information about you might make your résumé stand out – and having common interests with potential employers or colleagues may be to your benefit.

Instructions

You will see instructions on signs in public places, in recipe books, in operating manuals, on packets of food, and a variety of other places.

Instructions are generally **written using the imperative form** of the verb. The imperative is formed by using the infinitive form of the verb without *to*:

> *Keep off the grass*
> *Stop at the white line when light shows red*
> *Now add the garlic and tomatoes*
> *Shake before use*
> *Reconnect the plug to the power outlet*

Negative imperatives are generally formed by putting *do not* or *never* before the verb:

> *Do not open door while machine is operating.*
> *Do not leave in bright sunlight.*
> *Never leave small children unattended.*

Notice that sentences that give instructions often leave out words that you would find in ordinary sentences. For example, they sometimes do not include articles (*the* or *a*). Sometimes they leave out objects. For example, the sentence above reads, "Do not leave in bright sunlight." It does not say "Do not leave *this item* in bright sunlight."

> **Key point to remember**
> Instructions are generally not written as complete sentences and they do not show *who* must follow the instruction.

Think carefully about your readers before you start to write your instructions. Consider:

- How much or how little do they know about the task for which you are writing instructions?

- How old are they?

The answers to these two questions will help you to decide:

- The level of your instructions and **how many steps you include**. If the reader knows little or nothing about the task that you are describing, you may need to give instructions for every action that is required, even if some of the instructions seem very simple to you.

- How **simple or difficult the language of your instructions is**. Will they, for example, understand technical terms? If not, you will have to find a way of giving instructions that involves simple language that anyone could understand.

- Whether you need to **add warnings to your instructions** for younger readers. For example, in a recipe you may need to warn the reader that a food is hot at a particular point and they must not touch it. Or you may decide to tell the younger reader to ask an adult for help with a particular action.

When you are writing instructions, make sure that they are **easy to follow**. Make them as **clear** and as **simple** as possible. Remember that the reader will be using your instructions because they have not done a particular task before.

Use **short, simple sentences**. Long sentences are hard to follow and can confuse the reader. Compare the following instructions for making chocolate refrigerator cake:

Recipe 1
Melt butter in pan and add cocoa, sugar, and syrup, bringing to a boil, then remove from heat and stir in broken cookies, mixing well. Press mixture into pan then melt chocolate in microwave, (medium power for 15 seconds), spreading the chocolate when melted evenly over the surface using a knife and refrigerate before slicing.

Recipe 2
1 Melt butter in pan.
2 Add cocoa, sugar, and syrup to pan and bring mixture to a boil.
3 Remove from heat and stir in broken cookies. Mix well.
4 Press mixture into pan.
5 Melt chocolate in a microwave (medium power for 15 seconds).
6 Spread melted chocolate evenly over the surface using a knife and refrigerate before slicing.

Recipe 1 is confusing and difficult to follow for the following reasons:

- It uses long sentences. It gives you ten instructions in just two sentences. This is too much information for the reader to take in.

- It gives some instructions in a form that is not the imperative. For example, it uses the -ing form of the verb *bring* in "bringing to a boil" and not the clearer "bring to a boil."

- It relies on words such as *then* and *and* to tell the reader the order in which they should do different things. This is hard for the reader to understand and remember.

Recipe 2 is clear and easy to follow:

- It breaks up the ten instructions into seven short sentences in a numbered sequence.

- The reader can easily see the order of those instructions as each new step starts a new line.

- It uses the imperative form (melt the butter, remove from heat, press mixture, etc.), for every instruction.

> **Key point to remember**
> Avoid using the passive form ("be verb-ed") when writing instructions. The active form is clearer:
>
> ✗ The red button is pressed to start the wash cycle.
> ✔ Press the red button to start the wash cycle.

It is helpful to **give instructions as a list** rather than a paragraph. A list clearly separates the different actions that the reader must do and makes the instructions easier to follow. Your list may be numbered, or may have bullets:

Bake from frozen in 15 minutes
1 Preheat oven to 400°F.
2 Remove all packaging.
3 Place in the middle of oven and bake for 12-15 minutes.

Planting your seeds
- Fill a pot with compost.
- Spread the seed over the compost surface.
- Water the compost generously.

Think about the order of the actions that you are describing. Always give instructions for actions in the order in which you would perform them. This is not always as obvious or as easy as it sounds! Some actions can be performed at different stages of a task. Try to work out the most logical point at which to perform such actions. It can be helpful to write each step of a task on a different Post-it® note. You can then move the notes around until you have decided the most sensible order.

Consider **giving a title to your list of instructions**. The title should explain what the reader will achieve by following your instructions. You may want to make this sound exciting and appealing, especially if you are writing for children:

> *How to make the best chocolate brownies ever!*
> *How to make a mask that will scare your mom and dad!*

You may be writing instructions for a number of different but related tasks, for example, the different functions of a piece of equipment. It is useful here to **give short titles** for the various tasks, explaining what your instructions will help the reader to do. Note that the -*ing* form of the verb is usually used for titles like these:

> *Setting the gentle wash cycle*
> *Resetting/Changing the cycle*
> *Cleaning the appliance*

If the reader needs any items in order to perform your instructions, it is useful to **give a list of these items** before the instructions:

You will need:
2 pieces poster board (8" x 10")
glue
2 lengths thin ribbon (width 1/4")
sequins

Use helpful pictures or diagrams. Pictures and diagrams are especially useful:

- if the task for which you are giving instructions needs the reader to use different pieces of equipment or complicated equipment

- if you are writing for children

Choose your **pictures carefully**. Pictures or diagrams that are well-chosen and clearly labeled will show the reader immediately what things look like. (It can be difficult to describe in words the appearance of a particular thing or part.) They will also show how big or small one thing is compared with another thing. This can help to make sense of instructions. Make sure that your pictures or diagrams are:

- **clear and large enough** for the reader to see all the important parts

- **clearly labeled**. If you are using lines to point to different parts of a picture, make sure the reader can see exactly which parts of the picture the lines are pointing to.

> **Tip for success**
> Give the right number of labels. Label the parts that the reader needs to know about but do not label every part.

You may find it helpful to **test your instructions** to make sure that they work. Test your instructions on people who have not seen your instructions before or have not done the task that you are describing. This will show you:

- where your instructions are not clear

- where you have left out an important step or piece of information

Choose the people to test your instructions carefully – they should be typical of the sort of person who will be using your instructions. To learn the most from this activity:

- ask the person or people to read through your instructions carefully and then ask them if they have any questions or comments

- ask questions that will show whether they have understood your instructions

- if possible, watch the group try to perform the task by following your instructions. Afterwards, ask them how easy they found the task. Were there any instructions that they found confusing?

You can then rewrite any part of your instructions that was not clear or give instructions for any part of the task that was missing.

Leaflets and flyers

A leaflet or flyer is a printed sheet of paper that gives information about something. Leaflets are given to a large number of people free of charge.

Leaflets do a variety of things. They may simply give information, for example, on a particular health problem, on an event or sale, or on garbage collection in a particular area. They may try to persuade people to buy a particular product or service, or they may try to persuade people to have a particular belief.

Whatever the purpose of a leaflet, all leaflets have a few features in common. **Leaflets are small**. Most are just one sheet of paper, sometimes folded in two or three. (This is necessary as they will be picked up, quickly read, and often then put in a pocket or bag.) Consequently, leaflets generally contain **only the most important facts** on a particular subject and they **communicate those facts in just a few words**.

When you are writing and designing a leaflet, keep in mind that people generally **look at a leaflet very quickly**. Remember:

- Use large type to convey the most important information in a few words.
- Do not include information that is not important.
- Keep the text – or texts – short.
- Express your points clearly so that they are easy to understand.
- Include a telephone number/website address or other contact information.

Before you start to write your leaflet, **draw a rough sketch** of how you want it to look. Plan where you are going to put the title, the words, and any pictures you are using.

Try to make the leaflet look attractive and choose an image or images that will capture people's attention. **The right image or images** will also **help to communicate your message**.

Do not put too much in your leaflet. Remember that people need to be able to read a leaflet quickly. If they think that your leaflet will take them too long to read, they may not even pick it up! **Leave plenty of white space** around the text and images.

You can design your leaflet in a number of ways, even if it is a single-page leaflet. For example, you could put just a title and image on the front of the leaflet and the words themselves on the back. You may decide to put both images and text on both sides of the leaflet. **Make these important decisions before you even start to write the text.**

> **Tip for success**
> Before you do anything else, plan the overall design of your leaflet.

When you have prepared an overall design for your leaflet, it is time to choose the words. The best way to do this is to try to **see those words through the reader's eyes**. Imagine the questions the reader might ask when they pick up your leaflet.

Your first task, therefore, is to work out **who your typical reader is**. It is only when you have worked this out that you can start to work on the words.

For example, imagine you are preparing a leaflet for a cooperative that delivers boxes of organic fruit and vegetables to people's houses. The typical reader is a person who has at some point considered having a box like this delivered. The reader now wants to find out how your particular cooperative would provide such a service. You can assume that the reader is interested in this type of service because one or more of these is true:

- They like good quality food.
- They care about the environment.
- They want to support small, independent companies.

They will therefore probably want answers to the following questions:

- How good is the food?
- Is it truly organic?
- How eco-friendly is the cooperative?
- Who runs this cooperative?

On the basis of these questions, the facts that you would want to include in your leaflet are:

- The food is of the highest standard – fresh and delicious.
- The food is grown according to strict organic standards, without pesticides.
- The cooperative respects the environment in everything it does, for example in using only crops grown locally and in using very little packaging.
- This is a small, locally organized cooperative.

Other facts that *any* reader will want to know are:

- How much does it cost? (Are there different prices for different size boxes?)
- How convenient is it? (Can I choose what fruit and vegetables I have in my box?)

What is important is that you **remember to keep the reader's needs in mind**. *Only* include information that is interesting and useful to them. *Do not* be tempted to give a lot of detailed information.

Tip for success
Before you include information in your leaflet, ask yourself these two questions:

Will the reader want to know this?
Will the reader understand this?

When you know what information you want to include in your leaflet, you must decide how you are going to present that information. A bulleted list **is a very clear way of presenting key information**. Look at the text in the following leaflet:

> Greener Gardening – Local Garden Service
>
> We do all types of gardening tasks, including garden design, hedge trimming, garden maintenance, lawn maintenance, flower beds, tree & shrub planting and grass cutting.

Now see how a bulleted list can make the same information much clearer:

> Greener Gardening – Local Garden Service
>
> We do:
> - Garden design
> - Hedge trimming
> - Garden maintenance
> - Lawn maintenance
> - Flower beds
> - Tree & shrub planting
> - Grass cutting

Your leaflet may include the type of information that you cannot present in a list. For example, you may need to explain a number of facts, requiring you to write a series of paragraphs. If you are including a lot of information, remember to **break up the text with titles** for the different paragraphs.

Look at the text in the following medical leaflet:

> Symptoms of the virus may include a sore throat, headache, fever,
> loss of appetite or extreme tiredness. Call your doctor immediately
> if you are pregnant or your condition suddenly gets much worse.
> Some people are more at risk of serious illness if they catch the virus.
> At risk are people with long-term lung disease, heart disease, and
> kidney disease.

Now see how titles can make the same information much clearer:

> **Common symptoms**
> Symptoms of the virus may include a sore throat, headache, fever, loss
> of appetite, or extreme tiredness.
>
> **Call your doctor immediately if:**
> You are pregnant or your condition suddenly gets much worse.
>
> **High-risk groups**
> Some people are more at risk of serious illness if they catch the virus.
> At risk are people with long-term lung disease, heart disease, and
> kidney disease.

Get your reader's attention from the start. Make the first line of your
leaflet count. For example, rather than starting the text by describing
your company, you could present the reader with the problem that your
product or service will solve. Look how one home-delivery pizza
company starts their leaflet:

> *Sandro's Pizzas*
> *We deliver hot, tasty pizzas within a two-mile*
> *radius of Lockport.*

Now see how effective it can be to take a different approach, talking directly to the reader:

> *Paolo's Pizzas*
> *Hungry but had enough of cooking? We deliver*
> *hot, tasty pizzas …*

Include quotations. If you are trying to sell a product or service with your leaflet, you may like to include quotations from previous satisfied customers (though first check with the customer that they are happy for this to happen!):

> *"The most delicious, authentically Italian pizzas*
> *I've ever eaten in this country!" (K Santini, Lockport)*

Use simple language. Keep the language of your leaflet simple. Never include technical terms that your readers may not know. Make the sentences short so that the leaflet can be read and understood quickly.

Provide the right contact details. Will the readers of your leaflet want to call you or go to your website? Do they need to know where your office is or how to email you? Make sure you provide the contact details that your reader needs. Include an area code with any telephone number, and full address details. Even if your leaflet is to be distributed locally; you don't know who might pick it up, or where it might travel to.

Make your contact details clearly visible. Write them where the reader will see them. The top or bottom of a leaflet is usually clearer than the middle of a piece of text. Consider writing them on *both* sides of the leaflet.

Edit your leaflet. Remember that your leaflet is going to be read by members of the public and you need to create the best possible impression. The spelling, grammar, and punctuation in your leaflet must therefore be perfect. Read and reread your finished leaflet. If possible, have someone else check it.

Test your leaflet on a friend or colleague. Show them your leaflet for ten seconds only. Now ask them two questions (getting the answer for the first question before you ask the second):

1 What was the main purpose of the leaflet?
2 Tell me three things you have learned from the leaflet.

Could your friend/colleague tell you the main purpose of the leaflet? Were the three things they learned from the leaflet the three *key* things that you want your readers to notice? If their answers were not what you were hoping for, consider rewriting parts of your leaflet.

> **Tip for success**
> Take time to prepare your leaflet properly. A badly written leaflet may do more harm than good, no matter how many people read it.

Grammar, punctuation and spelling

PART THREE

Main verbs

Verbs are words that allow us to talk about activities, processes, states of being, and states of mind.

> This basket **holds** quite a lot.
> John **was reading** Katherine's essay.
> Anirban **is preparing** a talk for next week's class.
> Eleni **feels** much happier now.
> I **forgot** that it was your birthday.
> Paul **owned** several old motorbikes.

A **verb phrase** can be a single word or a group of connected verbs:

> he **walks**
> he **is walking**
> he **had walked**
> he **can walk**
> he **has been walking**
> he **might have been walking**

Transitive verbs are verbs that have an object:

> like: She **likes** cheese. (You can't say just "She likes.")
> describe: He **described** the house. (You can't say just "He described.")

Intransitive verbs do not have an object:

> sneeze: I **sneezed** loudly. (You can't sneeze *something*.)
> complain: He's always **complaining**. (You can't complain *something*.)

Many verbs can be **transitive or intransitive** – usually with slightly different meaning:

> *Sales levels have **increased**.* (Intransitive.)
> *We have **increased** our spending on training.* (Transitive.)
> *The fog made it difficult to **see**.* (Intransitive.)
> *The fog made it difficult to **see** the mountains.* (Transitive.)

The **infinitive** form of the verb is the basic form that you would look up in a dictionary. For instance, if you wanted to look up the verb in this sentence,

> *She had **encountered** many problems.*

you would look up the **infinitive**, *encounter*, not *encountered*. In different situations, the infinitive is used with or without *to*. Without *to*, it is called the **bare infinitive**:

> *The child was too small **to reach** the switch.*
> *I'm sorry **to hear** your news.*
> *Let her **do** it by herself.*
> *You must **lock** the door.*

Auxiliary verbs

Auxiliary verbs are used with main verbs in order to allow us to talk about different periods of time and to form questions and negatives.

Be and **have** are the **primary auxiliaries**. A primary auxiliary is used to construct compound tenses.

Be is used to make present continuous and past continuous tenses and for the passive:

> I **am working**.
> We **were** all **wondering** about that.
> Martin **was arrested** and held overnight.

Have is used to make present perfect and past perfect tenses:

> Sasha **has finished** fixing the car.
> Amanda **had** already **eaten** when we arrived.

Do is the **supporting auxiliary**. It is used in forming negatives, questions, and emphatic statements:

> I **do** not **like** sausage at all.
> **Do** you **like** shrimp?
> You **do like** shrimp, don't you?

Tip for success
In speech and informal writing, the auxiliary verbs *be* and *have* often join with their main verb to make a contraction, e.g., *I'm, she's, they've.*

Modal verbs

Modal verbs are used before other verbs to express ideas such as ability, possibility, and necessity.

The main modal verbs in English are:

can	could	may	might	must
ought	shall	will	would	

Modal verbs are different from other verbs because they do not change their form:

> I **can** ride a horse
> She **can** ride a horse.

In speech and informal writing, the modal verb **will** is often shortened to **'ll** (e.g., *I'll, they'll*) and the modal verb **would** is often shortened to **'d** (e.g., *I'd, they'd*).

Negatives of modal verbs are formed like this:

modal verb	negative	short form
can	cannot	can't
could	could not	couldn't
may	may not	mayn't (not used in modern American English)
might	might not	mightn't
must	must not	mustn't
ought	ought not	oughtn't
shall	shall not	shan't (rarely used in modern American English)
will	will not	won't
would	would not	wouldn't

Phrasal verbs

A phrasal verb is a type of verb that is created when a main verb is combined with either:

- an **adverb:**

    take off   *give in*
    blow up   *break in*

- a **preposition:**

    get at (someone)   *pick on (someone)*

- or an **adverb + preposition:**

    put up with (something)   *get out of (doing something)*

Often the meaning has nothing to do with the literal meaning of the verb or the particle (the adverb or preposition).

Tip for success
Nouns formed from phrasal verbs (e.g., takeoff, breakin) normally don't have hyphens. Use a space rather than a hyphen between the parts of phrasal verbs.

Nouns

A noun is a word that labels a thing or an idea.

Proper nouns are the names of people, places or things, and start with capital letters:

> *John Lennon*   *China*   *Mount Everest*   *Thursday*

Common nouns are all the other nouns that refer to things. They can be divided into the following groups:

- **Abstract nouns**. These refer to things that you cannot see or touch:

  > *honesty*   *anger*   *idea*   *time*

- **Concrete nouns**. These are things you can see or touch:

  > *dog*   *teacher*   *stone*   *sugar*

A concrete noun may refer to a living thing (**animate** noun) or a physical object (**inanimate** noun).

Collective nouns refer to collections of people or animals:

> *a **herd** of cows*
> *a **swarm** of bees*

Compound nouns are nouns made from two or more words. Some are written as one word, some as two words, and some with hyphens:

> *teapot*   *washing machine*   *son-in-law*

Many compound nouns have more than one acceptable form (e.g., stomach ache/stomachache). Check in a dictionary if you are not sure.

Countable and uncountable nouns

Countable nouns refer to things that we can count: *one cat, two cats, seventeen cats*, and so on. They have singular and plural forms, which are shown by the spelling. They must be used with a determiner (see below) if they are singular:

>***Dogs** ran wild in the streets.*
>***The dog** is loose again.*
>*Get **a chair** for Sumit, will you?*
>*We've bought **six new chairs**.*

Uncountable nouns refer to things that we cannot count:

>*Sadia asked me for some **advice**.*
>*Anna gave us some more **information** about her **work**.*
>***Homework** occupied much of Sonia's evening.*
>*Our **knowledge** of outer **space** is increasing daily.*

Uncountable nouns do not usually have a plural form. They are followed by a singular verb. They are not normally used with the indefinite article. (You cannot talk about "an advice" or "a money.")

Mass nouns refer to substances that can be divided or measured but not counted. They do not usually have an indefinite article in front:

>***Meat** is usually more expensive than **cheese**.*
>***Sugar** is quite cheap.*

Mass nouns only take a plural in special cases: for instance, when they refer to a particular type or types of the substance, or when they refer to a serving of the substance:

>*Rosa brought out a tempting selection of **French cheeses**.*
>***The principal sugars** are glucose, sucrose, and fructose.*
>***Two teas**, please.*

Pronouns

A pronoun is a word that is used instead of a noun phrase or a noun. We use pronouns when we do not want to repeat the same noun in a sentence or paragraph:

> Gary saw Sue so **he** asked **her** to help him.
> Costas was hungry so **he** stopped at a burger joint.

There are seven different types of pronoun, classified according to their meaning and use.

Personal pronouns can be used as subject or object in a clause:

> **He** gave **her** a box of chocolates.
> **We** saw **them** both on Friday.
> **I** can see **you**!

Reflexive pronouns are used when the action of a verb is performed on the subject by the subject. They are obligatory with certain verbs:

> The puppy entangled **itself** in the **leash**.
> I've just cut **myself** on a piece of glass.

Reflexive pronouns are also used for emphasis:

> Never mind. I'll do it **myself**.
> The professor **himself** did not know the answer.

Possessive pronouns indicate ownership:

> Give it back, it's **mine**.
> Perhaps it really is **theirs** after all.

> **Tip for success**
> Note that possessive pronouns are never spelled with an apostrophe. Avoid the common mistake of writing *it's* for the possessive form. *It's* is a short form for *it is*.

Demonstrative pronouns indicate items that are near to or far from us:

>*This* is Betty's and *that* is Peter's.
>*These* are nice. Where did you find them?

Relative pronouns are used to link a modifying clause (the part of a sentence that gives more information about a word or phrase) to a noun phrase or to a clause:

>I don't know *what* you mean.
>That's the girl *who* always comes top.

Interrogative pronouns are used to ask a question about the noun phrase they stand in for:

>*What* would you like for lunch?
>*Which* is the fresh milk?
>*Who* was responsible?

Indefinite pronouns are used for a broad range of reference when it is not necessary or not possible to use a personal pronoun:

>*Everyone* had a compass and a whistle.
>*Neither* wanted to give in and apologize.
>*Much* needs to be done.

Personal pronouns have **subject forms** (*I, you, he, she, it, we, they*) and **object forms** (*me, you, him, her, us, them*). It can sometimes be difficult to decide which to use, especially when you need to use two pronouns or a personal noun and a personal pronoun together. Here are some rules:

- If they are the joint *subject* of the verb, the subject form of the pronouns must be used:

    Jerry and I are going to paint the house ourselves.
    He and I are going to paint it.
    Melanie and I are going shopping.

> **Tip for success**
> Avoid the common mistake of saying, for example,
> **Jerry and me are ...**

- If they are the joint *object* of the verb, the object form of the pronouns must be used:

    They decided to help Jane and me.
    I want to give you and him a present.

> **Tip for success**
> Some people try too hard to be correct and make the mistake of saying, for example, "They decided to help Jane and I." If you are not sure which pronoun to use, imagine you were only using one of them. You would never write "They decided to help I," so if you remember that, you will choose the correct pronoun.

- The object form of pronouns must be used after prepositions:

  *Between **you and me**, I don't like this place.*
  *Wasn't that kind of **him**?*

You should follow the rules above, but in some situations the rules on subject and object pronouns are changing. In the following situations, it is now considered acceptable to use object pronouns, and using subject pronouns sounds extremely formal or old-fashioned:

- after the verb *be*.

  *I saw at once that it was **her**.*
  *I saw at once that it was **she**.*   Formal/old-fashioned

- after *than* in comparison with *be*.

  *Sylvia is smarter **than me**.*
  *Sylvia is smarter **than I**.*   Formal/old-fashioned

Adjectives

An adjective gives more information about a noun. Adjectives help us describe or pick out which particular thing among many is being referred to.

a man	*a **tall** man*
their TV	*their **new**, **wide-screen** TV*
the cat	*the **fat**, **black-and-white** cat*

When there is more than one adjective, commas are often used between them, though it is common to see lists of adjectives without commas too. It is possible to use several adjectives at once, but in practice more than four is uncommon:

*a **happy young blonde Midwestern** girl*
***charming old rustic** log cabins*

The **comparative** form of an adjective is used to compare two people, things or states:

*Anna is **taller** than Mary, but Mary is **older**.*

The **superlative** form is used for more than two people, things, or states, where one of them has more of a quality than all the others:

*That is the **smallest** camera I have ever seen.*

There are two ways in which the comparative and superlative forms of adjectives are formed:

- You add **-er** (comparative) or **-est** (superlative) to the adjective. Adjectives with one syllable usually take these endings:

	comparative	*superlative*
bright	**brighter**	the **brightest**
long	**longer**	the **longest**
sharp	**sharper**	the **sharpest**

If the word already ends in **-e**, the **-e** must be left off. If a word ends in **-y**, it usually takes **-er** or **-est**, and the **-y** changes to **–i**:

	comparative	*superlative*
wise	**wiser**	the **wisest**
pretty	**prettier**	the **prettiest**
weary	**wearier**	the **weariest**

> **Tip for success**
> If you add **-er** or **–est** to adjectives of one syllable ending in a short vowel plus a consonant, you must double the final consonant, e.g., *bi**gg**er*, *sa**dd**est*.

- You add the word **more** or **most** in front of the adjective. Adjectives with three syllables or more use **more** or **most** in front of them:

	comparative	*superlative*
fortunate	**more** fortunate	the **most** fortunate
relevant	**more** relevant	the **most** relevant

Adjectives formed from participles (forms of verbs) use **more** or **most** as well:

	comparative	*superlative*
provoking	**more** provoking	the **most** provoking
enthralled	**more** enthralled	the **most** enthralled

Adjectives with two syllables (including those that already end in *-er*) can follow either pattern or sometimes both patterns. If you are doubtful about a two-syllable adjective, use the **more/most** pattern:

	comparative	*superlative*
shallow	**shallower** or **more** shallow	the **shallowest** or the **most** shallow
polite	**politer** or **more** polite	the **politest** or the **most** polite

A small group of irregular adjectives have quite different forms for the comparative and superlative forms:

	comparative	*superlative*
good	**better**	the **best**
bad	**worse**	the **worst**
far	**further**	the **furthest**

Remember that in formal English *more* or *-er* should be used to compare two people, things or states. It is common to see the superlative in sentences such as:

> *Tom and Sam are both twelve, but Tom is tallest.*
> *Which of the two sisters is most beautiful?*

However, in more formal writing, it is safer to use the comparative:

> *Tom and Sam are both twelve, but Tom is taller.*
> *Which of the two sisters is more beautiful?*

To indicate the opposite of both the *-er/-est* and the **more/most** forms of comparison, **less** or **least** is always used:

	comparative	superlative
sharp	**less** sharp	the **least** sharp
fortunate	**less** fortunate	the **least** fortunate
interesting	**less** interesting	the **least** interesting
involved	**less** involved	the **least** involved

Tip for success
Never try to use *more* and *most* and the *-er/-est* endings together. It is a common mistake to write things like "*the most cleverest person*," but this is not correct English.

Adverbs

Adverbs can sometimes be difficult to identify because the term *adverb* covers several quite different types of word. However, the basic characteristic of an adverb is that it gives information about the way that an action is carried out or when and where it takes place.

Most adverbs are formed by adding **-ly** to the end of the related adjective:

slow	slowly
clever	cleverly
annual	annually

Words that end in **-ble** drop the **-e** before **-ly** is added. So do the words *true* and *due*:

sensible	sensibly
suitable	suitably
true	truly
due	duly

> **Tip for success**
> A common spelling mistake is to add **-ley**. This mistake is often made when the adjective ends in the letter **-e**. Note the correct spelling of adverbs formed from adjectives ending in **-e**, e.g., extreme/extremely, divine/divinely, free/freely.

Adjectives that end in **-y** change to **-i** before adding **-ly**, unless, like *sly* or *dry*, they have only one syllable:

happy	happily
greedy	greedily
sly	slyly

Some adverbs keep the same spelling as the adjective to which they are related. It is often difficult to tell at first whether the word is an adjective or an adverb. The general rule is to look at the other words that it occurs with. If it comes before a noun it is probably an adjective:

> a **short way**   a **late meeting**
> a **long pause**   an **early lecture**

If it relates to a verb or an adjective it is probably an adverb:

> The lesson **was cut short**.
> We **met late** at night.
> Don't **stay long**.
> He **came in early**.

Sentence adverbs are used at the beginning of sentences or clauses. They can be adverbs ending in –ly or other adverbs, e.g., nevertheless, however:

> **Foolishly**, I gave him my address.
> **Actually**, I don't mind.
> **Nevertheless**, we must give him an answer.

Adverbs of degree are words like *rather*, *quite*, *somewhat*, *fairly*, *too* and *almost*, and they come before adjectives or other adverbs:

> She seems **rather** nice.
> Angela is a **very** good tennis player.
> She began to cry, **quite** loudly.

Some **adverbs of place** have the same spelling as prepositions. However, these adverbs do not have an object, and are often found at the end of a sentence or clause:

> *He rushed **in**.*
> *She hurried **over**.*
> *The two friends jumped **out**.*

Just like adjectives, some adverbs have **comparative and superlative** forms. These are usually formed with *more* and *most*:

> *Could you speak **more slowly**, please?*
> *Mrs. Kay's class behaved (the) **most reasonably**.*

To indicate the opposite of comparatives and superlatives, *less* and *least* are used:

> *I checked her work a bit **less thoroughly** this time.*
> *This product worked (the) **least effectively**.*

Note the adverb forms of *good* and *bad*:

adjective	adverb	comparative adverb	superlative adverb
good	well	better	best
bad	badly	worse	worst

Determiners

A **determiner** is used to point more precisely to the person, thing, or idea that is being talked about. Determiners make the reference of nouns more specific. If I say "**this** car" it is clear that I mean a particular car which is near me. If I change it to "**my** car" I am saying something specific about ownership.

Determiners include:

- The **indefinite article** (*a*) and the **definite article** (*the*).

- Words known as **demonstratives**, that show where something is, especially in relation to the speaker or writer: *this*, *that*, *these*, *those*.

- Words known as **possessives**, that show who or what something belongs to: *my*, *your*, *his*, *its*, *our*, *their*.

- Words known as **quantifiers**, that show the amount of something, e.g.: *some*, *any*, *few*, *enough*, *much*.

- **Cardinal numbers** (*one*, *two*, *three*, *etc.*) and **ordinal numbers** (*first*, *second*, *third*, *etc.*)

- Words known as **distributives**: *each*, *every*, *either*, *neither*.

- Words known as **exclamatives**, that are used in exclamations: *what*, *such*.

Prepositions

A preposition is one of a small but very common group of words that relate different items to each other. Most English prepositions have a number of meanings that are particular to each preposition.

Simple prepositions consist of one word, e.g., *in*, *on*, *under*. Complex prepositions consist of more than one word, e.g., *due to*, *together with*, *on top of*, *in spite of*, *out of*.

The list below shows all the common simple prepositions. Some words can be either **prepositions** or **adverbs**, depending on how they are used and what they combine with. A preposition needs an object, rather like a transitive verb. The words in *italics* are the prepositions that can also be used as **adverbs**.

> *aboard*, *about*, *above*, *across*, *after*, against, *along*, *alongside*, amid, among, *around*, as, at, atop, bar, *before*, *behind*, *below*, *beneath*, *beside*, *between*, *beyond*, by, despite, *down*, during, for, from, *in*, *inside*, into, like, minus, *near*, of, *off*, *on*, onto, *opposite*, *out*, *outside*, *over*, *past*, pending, per, plus, prior, pro, re, regarding, *round*, *since*, than, *through*, *throughout*, till, to, toward, *under*, *underneath*, unlike, until, unto, *up*, upon, via, with, *within*, *without*

In modern English, it is usually acceptable to end a sentence with a preposition, though in formal written English, you may want to avoid it:

> *That's the girl we were talking about.*
> (Acceptable for most forms of writing.)
>
> *That's the girl about whom we were talking.*
> (Very formal.)

Conjunctions

A **conjunction** joins two or more nouns or clauses to each other.

> *I went to the store **and** bought some bread.*
> *I bought some bread **but** I forgot to get the milk.*

In most formal writing, it is not considered good style to start a sentence with a conjunction. However, in more creative styles of writing, this is sometimes done for effect:

> *I did not expect him to give me any financial support. Or any support at all, for that matter.*

Tenses

Verb forms use tense to show the time of what you are writing about: in other words, whether it is in the past, the present, or the future:

> Jessica **works** in the post office.
> Laurence **worked** in the post office over the holidays.

There are two types of tense in English:

- **Simple tenses** consist of a single word.

- **Compound tenses** are formed using the present or past forms of auxiliary verbs with another verb ending in -*ing* or -*ed*.

These are the tenses in English:

Present simple

> I/we/you/they **play**
> he/she/it **plays**

Examples of the present simple are:

> I **go** to college in Bloomington.
> Manuela **sings** in a choir.

Past simple

> I/we/you/they **played**
> he/she/it **played**

Examples of the past simple are:

> I **cooked** a meal.
> He **saw** a tiger.

Future simple

> I/we/you/they **will play**
> he/she/it **will play**

Examples of the future simple are:

> We **will give** you the money.
> Louis **will call** you later.

Present perfect

> I/we/you/they **have played**
> he/she/it **has played**

Examples of the present perfect are:

> I **have ordered** a new sofa.
> This illness **has ruined** my life.

Past perfect

> I/we/you/they **had played**
> he/she/it **had played**

Examples of the past perfect are:

> They **had noticed** a strange smell.
> She **had visited** Biloxi before.

Future perfect

> I/we/you/they **will have played**
> he/she/it **will have played**

Examples of the future perfect are:

> We **will have finished** before dark.
> Jerry **will have done** his work by then.

Present continuous

> I **am playing**
> we/you/they **are playing**
> he/she/it **is playing**

Examples of the present continuous are:

> I **am waiting** for Jack.
> She **is finishing** her meal.

Past continuous

> I **was playing**
> we/you/they **were playing**
> he/she/it **was playing**

Examples of the past continuous are:

> We **were trying** to see the queen.
> The water **was splashing** all over the floor.

Tip for success
Be sure to use the correct form of the auxiliary verb.
It is not correct to say or write "We was trying ..."

Future continuous

> *I/we/you/they* **will be playing**
> *he/she/it* **will be playing**

Examples of the future continuous are:

> *Our choir* **will be performing** *in the cathedral.*
> *Mom* **will be worrying** *about us.*

Present perfect continuous

> *I/we/you/they* **have been playing**
> *he/she/it* **has been playing**

Examples of the present perfect continuous are:

> *We* **have been trying** *to phone you all morning.*
> *The snow* **has been falling** *all night.*

Past perfect continuous

> *I/we/you/they* **had been playing**
> *he/she/it* **had been playing**

Examples of the past perfect continuous are:

> *The children* **had been using** *my computer.*
> *Anna* **had been sitting** *there all day.*

Future perfect continuous

> *I/we/you/they* **will have been playing**
> *he/she/it* **will have been playing**

Examples of the future perfect continuous are:

> On Sunday, we **will have been living** here for 10 years.
> I **will have been working** on the project for over a year.

Regular and irregular verbs

Regular verbs form their past tenses with –ed:

> She wait**ed** for me.
> I look**ed** but I couldn't see her.

However, there are many common verbs that form their past tenses in a different way. Many of these have a different form for their simple past tenses and their compound past tenses. If you are not sure of the past form of a verb, check in a dictionary: the irregular ones will be shown.

Some examples of common verbs with irregular past forms are:

> become > became > become
> blow > blew > blown
> cost > cost > cost
> go > went > been
> leave > left > left
> swim > swam > swum
> take > took > taken

Subject, object and indirect object

The **subject** of a sentence is the person or thing that does the verb.
The subject can be a noun, a noun phrase or a pronoun:

> **Adam** played the piano.
> **The man in the blue coat** asked me some questions.
> **Her car** broke down.
> **They** forgot to buy any milk.

All sentences must have a subject.

The **object** of a sentence usually comes after the verb. It can also be
a noun, a noun phrase or a pronoun:

> I spilled **the milk**.
> She saw **a large, black bird**.
> We were able to fix **the broken shelf**.
> I couldn't find **it**.

Not all sentences have an object:

> She was riding. (No object.)
> She was riding a horse. (With object.)
> Erica was writing. (No object.)
> Erica was writing a letter. (With object.)

Some verbs also have another sort of object, called an **indirect object**.
An indirect object names the person or object for or to whom something
is done. It is usually needed with verbs like *give, find* and *owe*:

> Mike owes Tom **five dollars**.
> Naveen gave the dresser **a fresh coat of paint**.
> Susan bought her rabbit **some more food**.

Agreement

Agreement means making sure that all the words and phrases in a sentence have the correct form in relation to one another.

Subject/verb agreement

The form of the verb must be the correct one to go with the subject:

> *The house is very large.* (Singular subject, singular verb.)
>
> *The stars are very bright.* (Plural subject, plural verb.)

In very long sentences, it can be easy to make a mistake, especially if the verb is a long way from the subject.

If two singular subjects are joined by *and*, they need a plural verb:

> *Parminder and Amandeep **are** going on vacation.*
> *The table and the desk **need** polishing.*

However, if the two things joined with *and* are thought of as one thing, a singular verb is used:

> *Franks and beans **is** my favorite meal.*
> *Bed and breakfast **is** the cheapest form of accommodation.*

If the subject has *each*, *every*, or *no* before it, the verb should be singular, and the same is true for *any* before a singular subject:

> *Every seat **was** taken already.*
> *Each vase **holds** four or five roses.*

If two singular subjects are joined by *or*, *nor*, *neither/nor*, *either/or*, or *not only/but also*, a singular verb is used:

> *Neither Blake nor Jones **was** available for comment.*
> *Either Mrs. Spiese or Mr. Turner **takes** the children to practice.*

Titles of books, films, songs, etc. have a singular verb even if the title itself is plural:

> *"The Birds" is a really scary film.*
> *"Daffodils" was the first poem I learned in school.*

Pronoun agreement

Pronouns must have the correct form in relation to the things they refer to. Pronouns often refer back to another sentence:

> ***The car** started fine, but **it** broke down halfway to Memphis.*
> *I asked **Adam and Ella** to clean up their rooms. When **they** had finished, we went bowling.*

Singular subject followed by plural pronoun

Look at this sentence:

> *Any student who is going on the school trip should hand in their payment at the office.*

In this sentence, *any student* is singular, and the verb *is* is singular, but the plural pronoun *their* has been used.

Some people who have very strict rules on grammar would consider this to be wrong. However, this use of plural pronouns is widely accepted in modern English, especially because it allows us to avoid the clumsy use of *he/she* or *he or she*. It is OK to use in all but the most formal of documents, unless your teachers object to it.

Agreement with group nouns

Group nouns are words like *committee* or *parliament* that can mean the group or all the individuals in it. In American English, the singular form of the verb is usually used with group nouns.

> The army **was** marching toward us.

In British English, you can use either a singular or a plural verb with these nouns, but be sure to be consistent:

> The army **were** marching toward us.

Tense agreement

You must make sure that the tenses you use in a sentence or paragraph relate correctly to each other:

> While I was waiting, I **see** a film. (Incorrect.)
> While I was waiting, I **saw** a film. (Correct.)
>
> By noon, I **answered** over 50 emails. (Incorrect.)
> By noon, I **had answered** over 50 emails. (Correct.)

Be particularly careful when you use two or more modal or auxiliary verbs together. It is common to hear sentences such as:

> **I can** and **I have done it**.

This is incorrect because *can* cannot be used with *done*. The sentence should be:

> *I **can do** it and I **have done** it.*

Punctuation

The apostrophe (')

Misusing or omitting the apostrophe is one of the commonest punctuation errors.

Showing possession

The apostrophe (') is used to show that something belongs to someone. It is usually added to the end of a word and followed by an -s.

's is added to the end of singular words:

> a baby**'s** stroller
> Hannah**'s** book
> a child**'s** cry

's is added to the end of plural words not ending in –s:

> children**'s** games
> women**'s** clothes
> people**'s** lives

An apostrophe alone is added to plural words ending in –s:

> Your grandparents are your parents' parents.
> We're campaigning for workers' rights.
> They've hired a new ladies' fashion guru.

's is added to the end of names and singular words ending in –s:

> James**'s** car
> the octopus**'s** tentacles

However, an apostrophe only is often also used with names ending in -s, especially for more formal contexts or with famous names:

> *Dickens' novels*
> *Henry James' house*

's is added to the end of people or their names to indicate that you are talking about their home:

> *I'm going over to Harry's for tea tonight.*
> *I stopped by Mom's this afternoon, but she wasn't in.*

's can also be added to:

- whole phrases:

> *My next-door neighbor's dog was barking like mad.*
> *John and Kent's house was on TV last night.*

- indefinite pronouns such as *somebody* or *anywhere*:

> *Is this anybody's pencil case?*
> *It's nobody's fault but mine.*

- *each other*:

> *We're getting used to each other's habits.*
> *We kept forgetting each other's names.*

When the possessor is an inanimate object (rather than a living thing), the apostrophe is not used and the word order is changed:

> *the middle of the street* (not *the street's middle*)
> *the front of the house* (not *the house's front*)

To test whether an apostrophe is in the right place, think about who the owner is:

> the boy's books (= the books belonging to the boy)
> the boys' books (= the books belonging to the boys)

Key points to remember
An apostrophe is *not* used to form possessive pronouns such as *its*, *yours*, or *theirs*.
An apostrophe is *not* used to form the plurals of words such as *potatoes* or *tomatoes*.

With letters and numbers
An apostrophe is used in front of two figures referring to a year or decade:

> French students rioted in **'68** [short for 1968].
> He worked as a schoolteacher during the **'80s** and early **'90s**.

An apostrophe can be used in plurals of letters and numbers to make them more readable. It is also sometimes used to form the plurals of words and abbreviations spelled in all capital letters:

> Mind your p's and q's.
> His 2's look a bit like 7's.
> She got straight A's in her exams.
> There are six ATM's on campus.

Key point to remember
it's = it is, e.g., *It's a holiday today.*
its = belonging to it, e.g., *The dog was scratching its ear.*

Contracted forms

An apostrophe is used in shortened forms of words to show that one or more letters have been missed out. Contractions are usually shortened forms of auxiliary verbs:

be	**have**
I'**m**	I/we/they'**ve** (have)
We/you/they'**re** (are)	He/she/it/one'**s** (has)
He/she/it/one'**s** (is)	I/we/you/he/she/it/one/they'**d** (had)

would
I/we/you/he/she/it/one/they'**d** (would)

or the negative *not*:

not
We/you/they are**n't**
He/she/it/one is**n't**
I/we/they have**n't**
He/she/it/one has**n't**

In order to work out what the contracted forms '**s** and '**d** represent, you need to look at what follows them:

If '**s** is followed by an *-ing* form, it represents the auxiliary *is*.

> *She'**s reading** a book about the ancient Egyptians.*
> *He'**s going** to Puerto Rico for his vacation.*

If '**s** is followed by an adjective or a noun phrase, it represents the main verb *is*:

> *She'**s nervous** about meeting my parents.*
> *He'**s brilliant** at math.*

If **'s** is followed by a past participle, it can represent *is* as it is used in the passive:

>   He**'s portrayed** by the media as a kindly old grandfather.
>   It**'s** often **said** that rock stars are frustrated actors.

or *has* as it is used in the present perfect:

>   She**'s broken** her wrist.
>   It**'s been** ages since we last saw you.

If **'s** is followed by *got*, it represents the auxiliary *has*:

>   She**'s got** two brothers and one sister.
>   It**'s got** everything you could want.

If **'d** is followed by a past participle, it represents the auxiliary *had*:

>   I**'d raced** against him before, but never in a marathon.
>   She couldn't believe what she**'d done**.

If **'d** is followed by a base form, it represents the modal auxiliary *would*:

>   I**'d give up** now, if I were you.
>   When we were kids we**'d spend** hours out on our bikes.

If **'d** is followed by *rather* or *better*, it represents the modal auxiliary *would*:

>   We**'d better** go home soon.
>   I**'d rather** not talk about that.

The comma (,)

The comma marks a short pause between parts of a sentence.

Separating main clauses

Main clauses (main parts of sentences) that are joined together with *and* or *but* do not normally have a comma before the conjunction unless the two clauses have different subjects:

> *You go out of the door and turn immediately left.*
> *It was cold outside, but we decided to go out for a walk anyway.*

Separating subordinate clauses from main clauses

Commas are normally used if the subordinate clause (the part of the sentence that is not the main part) comes before the main clause:

> *If you have any problems, just call me.*
> *Just call me if you have any problems.*

Sometimes a comma is used even when the main clause comes first, especially if the clauses are particularly long:

> *We should be able to finish the work by the end of the week,*
> *if nothing unexpected turns up between now and then.*

Separating relative clauses from main clauses

Commas are used to mark off nondefining relative clauses. This is the type of clause that adds to information about a noun or noun phrase:

> *My next-door neighbor, who works from home, is keeping an eye on the house while we're away.*
> *She moved to Los Angeles, where she began her career as a singer-songwriter.*

Commas are not required in defining relative clauses (clauses that say who or what something is):

> *Let's make sure the money goes to the people **who need it most**.*
> *The computer **(that) I borrowed** kept on crashing.*

Separating items in a list

Commas are used to separate three or more items in a list or series:

> *She got out bread, butter, and jam* (but *bread and butter*).

Note that the comma is often not given before the final *and* or *or*:

> *They breed dogs, cats, rabbits and hamsters.*
> *We did canoeing, climbing and archery.*

Separating adjectives

Commas are often used between adjectives, whether they come before the noun or after a linking verb:

> *It was a hot, dry and dusty road.*
> *It's wet, cold and windy outside.*

A comma is not usually used before an adjective that is followed by *and*.

With adverbials

When an adverbial such as *however, therefore,* or *unfortunately* refers to a whole sentence, it is separated from the rest of the sentence by a comma:

> *However, police would not confirm this rumor.*
> *Therefore, I try to avoid using the car as much as possible.*

With sentence tags and short answers

Commas are used before question tags and after *yes* or *no* in short answers:

> *It's really cold today, isn't it?*
> *He's up to date with all his injections, isn't he?*
> *Are you the mother of these children? – Yes, I am.*
> *You're Amy Osborne, aren't you? – No, I'm not.*

With names

Commas are used to separate the name of a person or group being spoken to from the rest of the sentence:

> *And now, ladies and gentlemen, please raise your glasses in a toast to the happy couple.*
> *Come on, Olivia, be reasonable.*
> *Dad, can you come and help me, please?*

With discourse markers

Commas are used to separate discourse markers (spoken phrases, often with little meaning, that people use before or between parts of sentences) from the rest of the sentence:

> *Well, believe it or not, I actually passed!*
> *Now then, let's see what's on TV tonight.*
> *Actually, I really enjoyed it.*

In reported speech

Commas are used to follow direct speech (if there is no question or exclamation mark after the quotation), or to show that it comes next:

> *"I don't understand this question," said Peter.*
> *Peter said, "I don't understand this question."*
> *"You're crazy!" Claire exclaimed.*
> *"What do you think you're doing?" Dad bellowed.*

> It is also possible to punctuate reported speech of the type
> *Peter said, "…"* using a colon instead of a comma.
> *Peter said: "Dream on."*

In dates

A comma must be used between the day of the month and the year, when the two numbers are next to each other:

> *March 31, 2011*

Quotation marks (" ") or (' ')

Direct speech

Direct speech gives the actual words that a speaker used. It is common in fiction and other writing where the words of a speaker are quoted.

The words spoken are enclosed in double quotation marks:

> **"Have you been to the new shopping center yet?"** *enquired Shona.*
> **"I've already seen it,"** *John replied.*

The comma comes inside the quotation marks.

Other uses

Double quotation marks are also used:

- to indicate an unusual use of a word, or a word that is not familiar.

  She pointed out that websites used for internet voting could be **"spoofed."**

- to suggest that the writer wants to be distanced from a word or does not entirely accept the use of a word in the given context. These are sometimes called scare quotes.

  I think he's too broke to go away on vacation, but he insists on calling it a "staycation."

Single quotation marks are used:

- to draw attention to a word.

  The word **'book'** *can be used as a noun or a verb.*

- to set off a quotation within a quotation.

> *"I heard him say 'Wait for me' but when I looked back he was gone,"*
> *Lance said.*

Capital letters

A capital (also called upper case) letter is used to mark the beginning of a sentence.

When I was 20, I dropped out of university and became a model.

Capital letters are also used for the first letter in proper nouns. These include:

- people's names

  Jenny Fuentes   *William Daoudi*

- days of the week

  Wednesday   *Saturday*

- months of the year

  August   *January*

- public holidays

  Christmas   *Yom Kippur*

- nationalities

  Spanish   *Iraqi*

- languages

  Swahili   *Flemish*

- geographical locations

  Australia   *Loch Ness*
  Mount Everest   *the Mediterranean Sea*

- company names

  Dillard's   *HarperCollins*

- religions

  Islam   *Buddhism*

Capital letters are also used for the first letter in titles of books, magazines, newspapers, TV shows, films, etc. Where there are several words, a capital letter is usually used for all the main content words in the title (i.e. not the prepositions or the determiners – unless they are the first word in the title).

  The Times   *Harpers*
  Twelfth Night   *The Secret Garden*
  Newsweek   *Mamma Mia!*

The period (.)

Periods are used:

- to mark the end of a sentence

  Let's have some lunch.
  I have to catch a bus in ten minutes.

- to mark the end of a sentence fragment

  Are you cold? – Yes, a bit.
  Do you like this sort of music? Not really.

- in initials for people's names, although this practice is becoming less frequent

  J.K. Rowling   *George W. Bush*
  M.C. Hammer   *Warren G. Harding*

- after some abbreviations, although this usage is variable, especially with common abbreviations

  P.S. Stop in next time you're passing through.
  She's moved to the I.T. department.
  R.S.V.P. to Helen Douglas on 555 2938.
  The U.S. government reacted strongly to the accusation.

When an abbreviation consists of a shortened word such as *Re.* or *Prof.*, a period should be used.

  The Soc. of Retired Police Officers endorsed the decision.
  Prof. John Johansson will be speaking tonight.
  Flight UA 345: dep. 09:44 arr. 11:10.

When an abbreviation contains the last letter of the shortened word, a period is used.

> **Dr.** *McDonald*   **St.** *Mary's School*
> *41 Douglas* **Rd.**   *The Akron Bar* **Assn.**

Note that periods are not used in many common sets of initials:

> *Did you see that program on* **NBC** *last night?*
> *Millions of people now call the* **FBI** *crimestopper line each year.*

or at the end of headlines, headings and titles:

> *Fear grips global stock markets*
> *Teaching grammar as a liberating force*
> *Wuthering Heights*

Remember that a period, and not a question mark, is used after an indirect question:

> *He asked if the bus had left.*
> *I wonder what's happened.*
> *She asked him where he was going.*

In British English, the period is called a full stop.

The question mark (?)

The question mark shows the end of a question:

> *When will we be arriving?*
> *Why did you do that?*
> *Does any of this matter?*
> *He's certain to be elected, isn't he?*

Question marks are used in direct questions, i.e., when the actual words of a speaker are used. A reported question should end with a period:

> *The lady said, "Where are you going?"*
> *The lady asked where she was going.*

Note that you put a question mark at the end of a question, even if the words in the sentence are not in the normal question order, or some words are omitted. Care is needed here as such a sentence can look, at first sight, like a statement rather than a question:

> *You know he doesn't live here any longer?*

A period, rather than a question mark, is used after an indirect question:

> *I'd like to know what you've been doing all this time.*
> *I wonder what's happened.*

The exclamation point (!)

The exclamation point is used after exclamations and emphatic expressions:

> *I can't believe it!*
> *Oh, no! Look at this mess!*

> **Tip for success**
> The exclamation point loses its effect if it is overused.
> It is better to use a period after a sentence expressing
> mild excitement or humor.

> *It was such a beautiful day.*
> *I felt like such a fool.*

The colon (:)

The colon indicates a break between two main clauses which is stronger than a comma but weaker than a period.

A colon is used:

- in front of a list

    I used three colors: green, blue, and pink.
    Make sure you wear clothes made from natural fibers: cotton, silk, or wool.

- in front of an explanation or a reason

    Nevertheless, the main problem remained: what should be done with the two men?
    I decided against going away this weekend: the weather forecast was dreadful.

- after introductory headings

    Cooking time: about five minutes.
    Start time: 10 o'clock.

- to separate the hours from the minutes in expressions of time

    The conference call is scheduled for 10:45 this morning.

- in more formal writing, between two main clauses that are connected

    It made me feel claustrophobic: what, I wonder, would happen to someone who was really unable to tolerate being locked into such a tiny space?
    Be patient: the next book in the series has not yet been published.

- in front of the second part of a book title

    Farming and Wildlife: a study in compromise
    Beyond Single Words: the most frequent collocations in spoken English

- to introduce direct speech, especially when the quotation is particularly long

    He said: "You owe me three dollars and twenty-five cents."
    The US Defense Secretary said: "There was agreement within the administration that we didn't think we were far enough down the road toward getting control of nuclear weapons around the world to limit ourselves so explicitly."

The semicolon (;)

The semicolon is used to mark a break between two main clauses when there is a balance or a contrast between them.

Compare:

> *The engine roared into life. The propellers began to turn.*
> *The plane taxied down the runway ready for takeoff.*

with:

> *The engine roared into life; the propellers began to turn;*
> *the plane taxied down the runway ready for takeoff.*

A useful test to work out when to use a semicolon is to ask yourself whether the two clauses could be written instead as separate sentences. If the answer is yes, then you can use a semicolon.

Note that it is quite acceptable to use a period in these cases, but a semicolon is preferable if you wish to convey the sense of a link or continuity between the parts of your sentence:

> *I'm not that interested in jazz; I prefer classical music.*
> *He knew everything about me; I had never even heard of him.*

A semicolon is also used to separate items in a list, especially if the listed items are phrases or clauses, which may already contain commas:

> *The trip was a disaster: the flight was four hours late; the hotel,*
> *which was described as "luxury," was dirty; and it rained the*
> *whole week.*

Parentheses ( )

Parentheses are used to enclose a word or words that can be left out and still leave a meaningful sentence:

> *The wooded area (see map below) is approximately 4,000 acres.*
> *This is a process which Hayek (a writer who came to rather different conclusions) also observed.*

Parentheses are also used to show alternatives or options:

> *Any student(s) interested in taking part should email me.*
> *A goat should give from three to six pints (1.4 to 2.8 liters) of milk a day.*

Note that when the structure of the sentence as a whole demands punctuation after a bracketed section, the punctuation is given outside the parentheses:

> *I haven't yet spoken to John (I mean John Maple, my boss), but I have a meeting with him on Friday.*
> *For lunch we had sandwiches (pastrami on rye and so on), salami, coleslaw, fried chicken, and potato salad.*

Punctuation is given before the closing parenthesis only when it applies to the bracketed section rather than to the sentence as a whole:

> *He's very handsome (positively gorgeous in fact!) and still single.*

Brackets [ ]

Brackets, sometimes called square brackets, are used when supplying words that make a quotation clearer or that comment on it, although they were not originally said or written:

> *Mr. Runcie concluded: "The novel is at its strongest when describing the dignity of Cambridge [a slave] and the education of Emily [the daughter of an absentee landlord]."*

Square brackets with dots are used to show where some words have been left out:

> *Greg Smith, chief executive of Pharm-wise [...], addressed the meeting.*

Brackets are also used when you need to put a word or words in parentheses inside another set of parentheses.

> *The novel touches on aspects of colonial life in India (the author, E.M. Forster [1879–1970], visited there in the 1920s).*

The hyphen (-)

The hyphen joins words or parts of words.

Hyphens are used at the ends of lines where a word has been split, to warn the reader that the word continues on the next line. If the word you need to split is clearly made up of two or more smaller words or elements, you should put the hyphen after the first of these parts. Otherwise, you put the hyphen at the end of a syllable:

> *wheelbar-row*   *inter-national*
> *listen-ing*   *compli-mentary*
> *infor-mation*

It is best not to add a hyphen if the word is a short one, or if it would mean writing just one or two letters at the end or beginning of a line. For example, it would be better to write "unnatural" on the line below, rather than writing "un-" on one line and "natural" on the next.

Prefixes that are used in front of a word beginning with a capital letter always have a hyphen after them:

> *a wave of anti-Mexican feeling*
> *a neo-Byzantine cathedral*

A hyphen is used to join two or more words that together form an adjective, where this adjective is used before the noun it describes:

> *an up-to-date account*
> *a last-minute rush*
> *a six-year-old boy*

The hyphen is omitted when the adjective so formed comes after the noun or pronoun it describes:

> *The accounts are up to date.*
> *It was all rather last minute.*
> *He's six years old.*

Some common compound nouns are usually written with hyphens:

> *mother-in-law*   *great-grandmother*

Hyphens can be used to split words that have been formed by adding a prefix to another word, especially to avoid an awkward combination of letters or confusion with another word:

> *co-owner*
> *re-covering furniture*
> *the re-creation of battle scenes*

Dashes (–)

Printed books have two different kinds of dashes: the en dash (–) and the slightly longer em dash (—). These dashes can be created in most word processing programs on computers, but in fact most people just use a hyphen where printed books use an en dash, and two hyphens (--) where printed books use an em dash. The information below applies mainly to the way dashes are used in printed books and professionally edited text.

An en dash is used:

• to indicate a range.

> *pages 26–42*

• between two adjectives or noun modifiers that indicate that two countries or groups are involved in something or that an individual has two roles or aspects.

> *Swedish–Norwegian relations improved,*
> *the United States–Canada free trade pact*
> *a mathematician–philosopher*

• to indicate that something such as a plane or a train goes between two places.

> *the Anguilla–St. Kitts flight*
> *the New York–Montreal train*

An em dash is used:

- at the beginning and end of a comment that interrupts the flow of a sentence.

    Now children—Kenneth, stop that immediately!—open your books on page 20.

- to separate off extra information.

    Boots and shoes — all shapes, sizes and colors — tumbled out.

Spaces may or may not surround dashes; this is usually a matter of individual or prescribed style.

The slash (/)

The slash separates letters, words, or numbers. It is used to indicate alternatives, ratios and ranges, and in website addresses:

> *he/she/it*
> *200 km/hr*
> *the 2001/02 accounting year*
> *http://www.abcdefg.com*

Spelling

Why is spelling important?

Spelling in English is certainly not easy. Unlike with many other languages, it is often difficult to guess spellings from the way an English word sounds.

However, learning to spell well is important for good communication, and will help you with:

- **understanding other people**. If you are a confident speller, you will be able to read and understand written material easily and efficiently. Reading will probably be more fun, so you will read more. As a result, your reading, spelling, and writing are likely to improve.

- **making yourself understood**. If your writing is full of spelling mistakes, other people may find it hard to understand what you are trying to say. If a word is spelled incorrectly, they may struggle to work out which word you mean. If you are trying to persuade them to take your side in an argument, it may be more difficult to convince them. Poor spelling makes a piece of written work less appealing and less effective.

Whether we like it or not, other people judge us on the way we write. Although some people believe that spelling is not important and are not put off by mistakes in a piece of writing, many (if not most) people think that good spelling does matter.

Ways to improve your spelling

A good way to learn spellings is to use the "Look, Say, Cover, Write, Check" method:

- **Look** at the word carefully.
- **Say** the word aloud to yourself, listening to how it sounds.
- **Cover** the word and try to remember what it looks like.
- **Write** the word.
- **Check** what you have written to see if you have got it right.

Try **breaking the word up into its syllables** and sound them out, pronouncing even the silent letters:

> **dictionary** = dic + tion + ar + y
> **February** = Feb + ru + ar + y
> **handkerchief** = hand + ker + chief
> **business** = bus + i + ness

Look for patterns and relations between words. If there is a word you do not know how to spell, try to think of another word that is related to it, e.g., succeed/successful, govern/government.

Write words down to see if they look right. Often, if you write down two possible versions of a word, you will know which one is correct.

Read a lot. The more you read, the better you will become at noticing when a word is spelled wrongly.

Suffixes and prefixes

Suffixes are parts of words that are added to the end of a base word to make another word in that family, e.g., dark + -ness = darkness, happy + -ly = happily. Prefixes are added to the beginning of words, e.g., dis- + like = dislike, inter- + national = international.

There are several useful rules about adding suffixes and prefixes:

Adding a suffix to words that end with a silent *e*:
When you add a suffix that begins with a vowel, you drop the **e**:

> *abbreviate* + *-ion* = *abbreviation*
> *desire* + *-able* = *desirable*
> *hope* + *-ing* = *hoping*

Be careful, though. If the word ends in **ce** and sounds like **s**, or the word ends in **ge** and sounds like **j**, you do not drop the final **e**:

> *notice* + *-able* = *noticeable*
> *change* + *-able* = *changeable*
> *outrage* + *-ous* = *outrageous*

Adding a suffix to words that end with a consonant:
In words of one syllable ending in a short vowel plus a consonant, you double the final consonant when you add a suffix that begins with a vowel:

> *run* + *-ing* = *running*
> *thin* + *-est* = *thinnest*
> *swim* + *-er* = *swimmer*

In words of more than one syllable ending in a single vowel plus a consonant, if the stress is on the end of the word when it is pronounced, you usually double the final consonant when you add a suffix that begins with a vowel:

> begin + ing = beginning
> commit + -ed = committed
> occur + -ence = occurrence
> excel + -ent = excellent

When you add a suffix that begins with a vowel to a word that ends in a single vowel plus **p**, you usually double the **p**:

> kidnap + -er = kidnapper

When you add a suffix that begins with **e**, **i** or **y** to a word that ends in **c**, you add a **k** after the **c**. This is to keep the hard **k** sound when it is pronounced:

> mimic + -ed = mimicked
> picnic + ing = picnicking
> panic + -y = panicky

Adding a suffix to words that end with y:
When you add a suffix to a word that ends with a consonant plus **y**, you change the **y** to **i**:

> beauty + -ful = beautiful
> crazy + -ly = crazily
> happy + -ness = happiness

Some one-syllable words usually do not follow this rule:

> shy + -ly = shyly
> sly + -ly = slyly

Adding the ly suffix to words that end with *le*:
When you make an adverb by adding the suffix -**ly** to an adjective that ends with **le**, you drop the **le** from the adjective:

> *gentle + -ly = gently*
> *idle + -ly = idly*
> *subtle + -ly = subtly*

> **Tip for success**
> There are only three verbs in English that end in -ceed: *succeed, proceed, exceed*. All the others with that sound end in -cede, except the one English verb that ends in -sede: *supersede*.

Words ending in *ful*:
You always spell the suffix -**ful** with just one **l**, e.g.:

> *beautiful, faithful, grateful, hopeful, painful, cupful*

Words beginning with *al*:
When **all** and another word are joined to make a word without a hyphen, you drop the second **l**, e.g.:

> *all + ready = already*
> *all + though = although*
> *all + together = altogether*

Forming plurals

Making plurals of words that end with a consonant followed by *y*:
When you make a plural of a word that ends with a consonant plus **y**,
you change the **y** to **i** and add **–es**:

> fair**y** + -es = fair**ies**
> qualit**y** + -es = qualit**ies**
> stor**y** + -es = stor**ies**

Making plurals of words that end with a vowel followed by *y*:
When you make a plural of a word that ends with a vowel plus **y**,
you add **-s**:

> bo**y** + -s = boys
> da**y** + -s = days
> donke**y** + -s = donkeys

Making plurals of words that end with *s*, *x*, *z*, *sh* or *ch*:
When you make a plural of a word that ends with **s**, **x**, **z**, **sh** or **ch**,
you add **-es**:

> bus + -es = bus**es**
> fox + -es = fox**es**
> match + -es = match**es**

Making plurals of words that end with a single *o*:
When you make the plural of a word that ends with a single **o**,
you add **-s**:

> memo + -s = memos
> solo + -s = solos
> taco + -s = tacos

Be careful though, there are a few words that do not follow this rule.
If you have any doubt, check in your dictionary:

> *echo + -es = echoes*
> *hero + -es = heroes*
> *potato + -es = potatoes*
> *tomato + -es = tomatoes*

Making plurals of words that end with *f* or *fe*:

When you make the plural of a word that ends with *f* or **fe**, you often
have to change the **f** to **v**:

> leaf, *plural* leaves
> life, *plural* lives
> knife, *plural* knives
> loaf, *plural* loaves

Be careful though, there are a few words that do not follow this rule. If
you have any doubt, check in your dictionary:

> roof, *plural* roofs

Irregular plurals

Some plurals do not follow any of the usual rules. You just have to learn
them, or check in your dictionary if you are not sure.

Some words do not change at all in the plural:

> sheep, *plural* sheep
> aircraft, *plural* aircraft
> species, *plural* species

Some change in other ways:

>foot, *plural* feet
>mouse, *plural* mice
>analysis, *plural* analyses
>phenomenon, *plural* phenomena
>child, *plural* children

Compound words (words made of two or more words put together) follow the same pattern as that of their last part:

>grandchild, *plural* grandchildren

Alternative plurals

Some plurals have more than one possible form. Often one form is more formal or technical than the other, so you will want to think about the context in which you are using it. For example, you might use the more technical plurals in a scientific context.

>formula, *plural* formulas or (technical) formulae
>fungus, *plural* funguses or (technical) fungi

-ize or -ise?

The suffix **-ize** ends many English verbs and can be used to make new verbs out of nouns. This suffix is sometimes spelled **-ise** in British English, but never in American English.

Be careful, however, of some words that sound like they are spelled with **-ize** but in fact are always spelled with **-ise**. This is because these words have different histories and were not formed originally by adding the **-ize** suffix:

advertise	devise	revise
advise	disguise	supervise
chastise	excise	surprise
comprise	exercise	televise
compromise	franchise	
despise	improvise	

i before e except after c

This is a useful phrase to learn. It means that when **i** and **e** are put together to make the sound *ee*, the **i** comes before the **e**:

achieve	field	relief
brief	hygiene	siege
chief	niece	thief

However, when they follow the letter **c** in a word, the **e** comes before the **i**:

ceiling	deceit	receipt
conceive	deceive	receive

There are a few words that do not follow this rule:

caffeine	protein	seize

Silent letters

Some words contain letters that you do not pronounce, but it is still important to write them correctly, e.g.:

lamb   *sign*   *autumn*

Some words that begin with "ch" are pronounced "c":

character   *Christian*   *chemical*

Words that begin with "kn" are pronounced "n":

knee   *knife*   *knock*

Words that begin with "ps" are pronounced "s":

psychology   *pseudonym*   *psychopath*

Some words that begin with "sc" are pronounced "s":

scene   *scent*   *scientist*

Some words that begin with "wh" are pronounced "w" by most English speakers:

wheel   *where*   *white*

Words beginning with "wr" are pronounced "r":

write   *wrap*   *wrong*

Contractions

Contractions are formed when two or more words are put together, but part of at least one of the words is missing:

> don't = do not
> I'd = I would

We use an apostrophe to represent the missing letter or letters.

The most common contractions are of:

- **the verb *be*:**

   I'm, you're, he's, she's, it's, we're, they're

- **the verb *have*:**

   I've, you've, he's, she's, it's, we've, they've

- **the modal verb *would*:**

   I'd, you'd, he'd, she'd, it'd, we'd, they'd

- **the negative *not*, e.g.:**

   I can't
   we aren't
   they haven't
   she wouldn't

Common mistakes and controversial issues

Words that are often confused

Homophones

Homophones are words that sound the same but are spelled differently, and it is easy to become confused by them:

affect Affect is a *verb*: *How will this new law affect me?*	**effect** Effect is a *noun*: *What will the effect of the new law be?*
already Already is an *adverb*. If something has already happened, it has happened before the present time: *I've already called an ambulance.*	**all ready** In the phrase "all ready," *all* is a *quantifier* meaning the whole of a group or a thing, and ready is an *adjective*: *Are you all ready to go?*
alter Alter is a verb, meaning "to change": *Nothing in the house had altered since 1960.*	**altar** An altar is the holy table in a church: *The priest stood in front of the altar.*
anyone Anyone is a pronoun and always refers to people: *Has anyone seen my hat?*	**any one** In the phrase "any one", *one* is a pronoun or a determiner that can refer to a person or a thing, depending on the context: *We never stay long in any one place.* *It could have happened to any one of us.*
bare Bare is an adjective meaning "not covered" or "not wearing any clothes": *We ran along the beach with bare feet.*	**bear** A bear is a wild animal: *There are bears in the woods.*

board A board is a flat piece of wood: *They nailed a board over the window.*	**bored** If you are bored, you are not interested by something: *I was so bored at school today.*
capital Capital is usually a *noun*. It has several meanings, including a city that is also a seat of government: *Denver is the capital of Colorado.*	**capitol** Capitol is also a *noun*. It is a building where a legislature meets: *We took a tour of the capitol and other buildings at the civic center.*
cereal Cereal it is another name for grain, or for a food made from grain: *Do you eat cereal for breakfast?*	**serial** A serial is something that happens in or contains a series: *We watched a three-part serial about the life of Lincoln.*
chord A chord is a group of three or more notes played together: *Was that an A-minor chord?*	**cord** Cord is strong or heavy string: *Tie the package with some cord.*
coarse Coarse is an *adjective* meaning "having a rough texture" or "talking and behaving in a rude way": *The sand was very coarse.* *His manners are coarse.*	**course** Course is a *noun* with several meanings, including "a series of lessons" and "a route or path": *The plane changed course.* *I did a course in art history.*
compliment A compliment is a nice thing that someone says about someone or something. Compliment can also be used as a verb: *They paid him a lot of compliments.* *She complimented me on my roses.*	**complement** If people or things complement each other, they have different qualities that go well together: *The dry wine complements this rich sauce perfectly.*

counselor A counselor gives people advice, often on personal matters, as a job: *They went to see a marriage counselor.*	**councilor** A councilor is a member of a council: *She was elected as a councilor last year.*
discreet If you are discreet, you are careful to avoid attracting attention or revealing private information: *I made a few discreet inquiries about her.*	**discrete** If things are discrete, they are not joined or connected in any way: *I met him on three discrete occasions.*
everyone Everyone is a pronoun and always refers to people: *Everyone enjoyed the show.*	**every one** In the phrase "every one," one is a pronoun or a determiner that can refer to a person or a thing, depending on the context: *They have talked to every one of my classmates.* *We have eaten every one of the cookies.*
hoard If you hoard things, you save or store them for yourself: *She hoarded jars of fruit in the cellar.* Hoard can also be a *noun*: *We found a hoard of guns under the floorboards.*	**horde** A horde is a large crowd of people: *Hordes of shoppers crowded outside the store.*
hole A hole is an opening or a hollow space in something: *There's a hole in my shoe.*	**whole** Whole is a quantifier meaning "all of something": *He ate the whole loaf.*

its	**it's**
Its means "belonging to it": *The dog wagged its tail.*	It's means "it is" *It's going to be difficult to fit in all this work.*
led Led is the past participle of the verb *lead*: *He led me into a small room.*	**lead** Lead is a *noun*, meaning "a soft, gray metal": *The roof is covered with lead.* Lead is also a *verb*, but it has a different pronunciation.
libel Libel is a *noun* that denotes the crime of publishing lies about someone: *They sued the newspaper for libel.*	**liable** Liable is an *adjective* that means "legally responsible": *We are not liable for damage done to personal property.*
maybe *Maybe* is an adverb that modifies a verb, a predicate, or a whole sentence. There should always be a verb in a sentence that contains *maybe*: *Maybe I'll stay till they finish this set. I was standing maybe 30 yards away from the accident.*	**may be** May be is a verb phrase or part of the verb phrase in a clause; it is the modal verb *may* plus the infinitive *be*: *There may be other reasons for changing the date. You may be asked to provide a reason.*
pedal Pedal is a *noun* meaning the part of a bike you press with your foot, or a *verb* meaning to press that part: *Put your foot on the pedal. You'll have to pedal harder.*	**peddle** If you peddle something, you sell it: *He was caught peddling drugs.*

pray Pray is a *verb* that means "to speak to a god": *I prayed that they would arrive safely.*	**prey** Prey is a *noun* that denotes an animal eaten by another: *The lions are searching for prey.*
principle Principle is a *noun* meaning "a belief about what is right or wrong" or "a basic rule": *Eating meat is against my principles.* *We learned the basic principles of yoga.*	**principal** Principal is an *adjective* meaning "most important": *Bad weather was the principal reason for the failure of the expedition.* Principal can also be a noun meaning "the person in charge of a school": *She was sent to the principal's office.*
site A site is an area that is used for a particular purpose or where something happens: *He works on a building site.* *This is the site of the explosion.*	**sight** Sight is the ability to see, and a sight is something you can see: *She lost her sight in an accident.* *I faint at the sight of blood.*
stationery Stationery is a *noun* meaning "paper, envelopes and writing equipment": *Envelopes are kept in the stationery cupboard.*	**stationary** Stationary is an *adjective* meaning "not moving": *I drove into a stationary vehicle.*
straight Straight is an adjective meaning "not curved": *The road is straight for 20 miles, till the mountains start.*	**strait** Strait is a noun that denotes a narrow strip of water: *The ship was attacked in the Strait of Malacca.*

whether	**weather**
Whether is a *conjunction* used to talk about a choice or doubt between two or more alternative: *I can't decide whether to have soup or salad.*	Weather is a *noun* we use to talk about rain, snow, sun, etc.: *The weather was great in Florida.*
whose	**who's**
Whose is a *pronoun* and a *determiner* used to ask questions about who something belongs to, or to talk about things connected to a particular person: *Whose shoes are these?* *He helped a woman whose face was covered with blood.*	Who's means "who is" or "who has": *Who's going to do the dishes?* *Who's been sleeping in my bed?*
witch	**which**
Witch is a *noun*, meaning an evil magic woman: *We painted a witch on a broomstick.*	Which is a *pronoun* and a *determiner* used to ask questions when there are two or more possible alternatives, or to talk about things connected to a particular person: *Which is your cabin?* *I took the coat which looked warmest.*
your	**you're**
Your is a *pronoun* showing that something belongs to you or relates to you: *Where is your car?*	You're means "you are": *You're late again.*

Other words that are often confused

These words do not sound the same, but they are spelled in a similar way or related to each other, and often cause confusion:

accept Accept is a *verb* and means "agree to have": *I cannot accept money from you.*	**except** Except is a *preposition* and a *conjunction* meaning "not including": *Everyone was invited except Flora.*
adverse Adverse is a formal *adjective* meaning "bad" or "negative": *Do not attempt the climb in adverse weather conditions.*	**averse** If you are averse to something, you do not like it: *I'm not averse to a sing-along now and then.*
advice Advice is a *noun*: *Can you give me some advice about growing roses?*	**advise** Advise is a *verb*: *I advised him to wait a bit longer.*
beside Beside means "next to": *Put the chair beside the window.*	**besides** Besides means "as well" or "in addition to": *I don't need any help. Besides, I've nearly finished.* *He designed houses, office buildings, and much else besides.*
censure Censure is a formal verb, meaning "to criticize strongly." It is also a noun meaning the criticism: *They were censured for their failure to implement safety measures.* *The company received censure for its poor safety record.*	**censor** Censor is a verb meaning "to cut out parts of speech or writing." It is also a noun meaning the person who does this: *His letters home from the war were heavily censored.* *Government censors cut out much of what he wrote.*

continual Continual is used to mean that something happens without interruption, and also that something happens repeatedly: *I'm fed up with this continual noise.* *There have been continual demands for action.*	**continuous** Continuous is only used for things that happen without interruption and do not stop at all: *He has a continuous buzzing sound in his ear.*
definite If something is definite, it is firm and clear and not likely to be changed: *Do we have a definite date for the meeting?*	**definitive** Something that is definitive provides a firm, unquestionable conclusion: *No one has come up with a definitive answer.*
dessert A dessert is the sweet dish you eat at the end of a meal: *Shall we have a dessert?*	**desert** A desert is a large, dry sandy area: *We traveled through the Sahara Desert.* Desert (with the same pronunciation as dessert) is also a verb meaning "to abandon." *Settlers deserted the valley after one winter.*
elder Elder is used when you are saying which of two people was born first. It is not used with *than*: *I live with my elder sister.* *He is the elder of the two.*	**older** Older simply means "more old," and can be used of people or things, and can be followed by *than*: *My car is older than yours.*
flout If you flout a law or a rule, you do not obey it: *He accused the president of flouting international law.*	**flaunt** If you flaunt something, you show it off in an obvious way: *I saw her at the party, flaunting her jewelry.*

infer If you infer something, you draw a conclusion from what you have seen, heard or read: *From his resignation letter, I inferred that he had been forced to leave.*	**imply** If you imply something, you say it in an indirect way: *She implied that he owed her money.*
lay Lay is a *transitive* verb meaning "to put something somewhere carefully", and must have an object: *Mothers often lay babies on their backs to sleep.* It is not correct to say "I'm going to lay down" – you should use *lie* for this. Lay is also the past tense of *lie*: *We lay on the floor.*	**lie** Lie is an *intransitive* verb meaning "to be in a horizontal position": *I want to lie down.*
loose Loose is an *adjective* meaning "not firmly fixed": *The bolts had worked loose.*	**lose** Lose is a *verb* meaning "to not have something any more" or "to be defeated": *I'm always losing my keys.* *I think we're going to lose the match.*
personal Personal is an *adjective* meaning "private" or "relating to a particular person": *He asked me some very personal questions.* *She has her own personal helicopter.*	**personnel** Personnel is a *noun* meaning "the people who work in an organization": *All military personnel must report to base.*
quite Quite is a qualifying *adverb* that is used mainly in set expressions: *I haven't seen her for quite a while.* *Dinner is not quite ready.*	**quiet** Quiet is an *adjective* and describes things or people that do not make much noise: *She had a very quiet voice.*

These groups of three words are among the most commonly misused words in English. They are all extremely frequent, so it is important that you are confident about using them correctly.

they're	They're means "they are": *They're going to come on the train, I'll be angry if they're late again.*
their	Their is the possessive pronoun from "they": *They forgot to bring their coats.* *Their faces were white and tear-stained.*
there	There is a pronoun and adverb used to show position or direction, to show that something exists, and at the beginning of many sentences and phrases: *There's your jacket.* *Can you see the lion over there?* *The old buildings are still there today.* *There must be another way of doing this.* *There are three churches in our town.*
too	Too is used before adjectives to mean "more than is good": *It's too hot in here.* It also means "as well": *I want some too.*
to	To is a preposition that is used in many ways, but the main ones are showing direction, showing who receives something, and forming the infinitive: *We went to the zoo.* *I gave it to John.* *I need to buy a new coat.*
two	Two is the word for the number 2: *I have two brothers.*

we're	We're means "we are": *We're having a party.* *I'll phone you when we're there.*
were	Were is the past tense of *be* when the subject is plural: *We were very happy.* *They were going to tell you.*
where	Where is used to talk about the location of things or to ask questions about the location of things: *Where do you live?* *I left the keys where Kabelo would be sure to find them.*

Words that are often misspelled

These are words which people often misspell. A few of them are difficult words, but most of them are quite common, and it is important to spell them correctly.

accidentally	Don't forget -*ally* at the end, not just -ly.
accommodation	Double *c* and double *m*. This is one of the most commonly misspelled words in English.
acquire	Don't forget the *c* before the *q*.
advertisement	Don't forget the *e* after the *s*.
apparent	Double *p* but only one *r*.
beautiful	Learn the group of vowels – *eau* – at the beginning.
because	Remember *au* after the *c*.
believe	Remember *ie*, not ei.
Caribbean	Only one *r*, but double *b*.
catastrophe	Unusually for English, the final *e* is pronounced, but remember it is only one *e* – don't be tempted to write y or ee.
category	Remember it's *e* in the middle, not i or a.
cemetery	Remember that the first three vowels are *e*, there is no *a*.
definite/definitely	Remember that there are two *i*'s and no a's in this word.
desperate	The second vowel is *e*, not a (unlike *separate*).

different	Double *f* and don't forget the *e* after them.
discipline	Don't forget the *c* after the *s*, or the *e* at the end.
embarrassing	Double *r* and double *s*.
environment	Don't forget the *n* in the middle of this word.
especially	Remember that this word starts with *e*.
existence	This word ends -*ence*, not -ance.
foreign	Remember *ei* in the second syllable, and don't forget the *g*.
forty	Unlike *four*, there is no *u* in this word.
gauge	Remember the vowel sound is *au*.
government	Don't forget the *n* in the middle of this word. Remember that it comes from the word *govern*.
grammar	Remember that this word ends -*ar*, not -er.
guarantee	Remember the *u* in the first syllable of this word.
harrass	Remember: one *r*, double *s*.
independent	Remember that this word ends -*ent*, not -ant.
island	Don't forget the *s*.
leisure	Remember that in this word, *e* comes before *i*, which is the other way around from the usual rule.
library	Don't forget the *r* after the *b*.

lightning	Do not be tempted to add an e after *light*.
maintenance	Remember that the second vowel sound is made by *e* (even though the related verb is *maintain*).
maneuver	The vowel sequence *eu* has an unusual pronunciation in this word and it is easy to forget the *e*.
millennium	Double *l* and double *n*.
miniature	Don't forget the second *i*.
minuscule	Note that the second vowel is *u*, not i. Try to think of it as beginning with *minus-*, not mini-.
occurrence	Double *c* and double *r*.
opportunity	Double *p* and don't forget the *r* before the *t*.
possess/possession	Two lots of double *s*.
privilege	This is the most frequently misspelled word in English. Remember that the middle vowel is *i*, the last vowel is *e*, and there is no *d* (as there is in *knowledge*, for example). There are no a's in this word.
profession/professional/ professor	Remember there is only one *f* in these words.
pronunciation	Do not be tempted to add an o in the second syllable.
questionnaire	Remember to write double *n* in the middle.
receipt	Remember *ei* in the second syllable, and don't forget the silent *p*.

receive	Remember *ei* in the second syllable.
recommend	Only one *c* but double *m*.
relevant	Remember that the second vowel is *e*, not a.
restaurant	Remember to write *au* after the first *t*.
rhythm	This word is unusual in having two syllables, and none of the usual vowels. It's best to memorize the whole word.
seize	Remember *ei*, here not ie.
separate	Remember that the second vowel is *a*, not e.
truly	Do not be tempted to add an e after *tru*.
weird	Remember *ei*, not ie.

Common mistakes and controversial issues

The English language arouses strong emotions. Many people have very fixed ideas about what is wrong and what is right. It is important when you write – apart from very informal texts, emails, etc. – that you use a correct, standard form of English.

If you make mistakes such as putting apostrophes in the wrong place, or using the wrong form of a verb, your readers might be distracted from your message, and even take it less seriously.

It is important to remember that there are different customs for written and spoken English. While it might be acceptable in some situations to say something like "Jane and me are going shopping," nonstandard uses should be avoided in writing.

Several customs of English grammar have come about as a result of people applying the grammar of Latin to English. However, many people are inconsistent about this. For instance, someone who objects to the use of the word *data* as a singular noun (because it is plural in Latin), may be quite happy to use the words *agenda* and *stamina* as singular nouns, even though they are Latin plurals too.

Another important thing to bear in mind is that language changes. The language used by E. M. Forster writing in the 20th century is very different from that of Shakespeare writing in the 16th century, but nobody would say that Forster's English was incorrect.

New words and phrases come into the language all the time, and even the grammar and structure of our sentences changes. Today many more people speak English as a second language than as a first language and the ways that they speak and write are beginning to have an influence on the way that English is developing.

In the notes that follow, you will find guidance on what is acceptable and what is not acceptable in current American English. However, there are many issues where people disagree, and as always, it is important to think of your audience. The most important thing is to avoid slang, informal expressions, and loose grammar when you are writing reports, papers, or material for publication.

All right or alright?

Some people consider that *alright* is not a real word, and that *all right* should always be used. However, *alright* is very commonly used, particularly when representing speech. It may be best to avoid it in very formal writing.

Among or between?

If we are talking, for example, of dividing or sharing things, *between* is usually used when there are only two people or things, and *among* when there are more than two:

> *Nora and Doyin shared the bread between them.*
> *We distributed leaflets among the crowd.*

However, many people use *between* no matter how many things there are, especially after the verb *choose*:

> *It is difficult to choose between all the different styles.*

Amount and quantity

In formal writing, it is best to use these nouns only with uncountable or mass nouns:

> *There was a large amount of mud on the carpet.*
> *We bought a small quantity of gold.*

It is not good style in formal writing to say things like: *I've got a huge amount of apples.* For countable nouns, it is best to use *number*, or to rephrase the sentence, for example: *I've got a lot of apples.*

Awhile

Because it is an adverb, *awhile* normally works as an adverbial and takes the place of the phrase "for a while":

> *We waited awhile and then two buses came.*

Many people, however, use *awhile* as the object of the prepositions *for* and *after*. This usage is acceptable in fiction and informal writing but should probably be avoided in formal writing:

> *It looked like rain for awhile but then it cleared.*
> *After awhile we left the beach and went to the movies.*

Comprise

Comprise is a formal word, and should not be used with the preposition *of*, even though the similar words *consist* or *be composed* are followed by *of*:

> *The grounds comprise a large lawn and 20 acres of woodland.*
> *My cold remedy consists of lemon, honey and garlic.*
> *The committee is composed of members of the legal profession.*

Could of/should of, etc.

It is a very common error to write *of* after modal verbs such as *could*, *might*, *should*, or *would*. This is because in speech, it sounds as if that is what we are saying. However, the sound is really a contracted form of the verb *have* (*could've*, *might've*, *should've*, etc.). In formal writing it is best to avoid the contractions all together:

> We could have helped you if you had asked.
> You should have called for a taxi.

Dangling participles

Dangling participles occur when the subject of the main clause is not the subject of the modifying clause that contains a participle (usually a word ending in *-ing* or *-ed*).

Look at the following sentence:

> Coming home from work, my hat blew off.

Coming is a dangling participle here because its subject is not *my hat*. In formal writing, it would be better to say something like:

> As I was coming home from work, my hat blew off.

Here is an example of a dangling past participle:

> Loathed by his colleagues, we understood why he had been fired.

This is incorrect in formal writing, because the subject of the main clause is *we*, but the subject of the participle is *he*. It would be better to write something like:

> He was loathed by his colleagues, so we understood why he had been fired.

It is fine to use clauses with participles as long as the subject of the main clause matches:

Having seen the play before, I was happy to go again.

Data

Strictly speaking, data is the plural form of the Latin *datum*. Some people insist that it should be used with a plural verb:

The data were collected over several years.

However, data is often used as a singular noun, and most people would accept that as a valid use. There is some logic to this too, since data is often used as a synonym for *information* or *evidence*, which would take singular verbs:

All the data was uploaded to the new server.

Data tends to be used as a plural more commonly in scientific or academic writing. Whether you decide to use a singular or a plural verb with data, make sure that you are consistent throughout your document.

Decimate

This word originated from the Roman custom of killing one in ten of a group of soldiers guilty of crimes such as mutiny. A few people, therefore, prefer to use decimate very specifically to mean "to reduce by one tenth."

However, in modern English, decimate is used to mean "to destroy a large amount or number of something" and this is widely acceptable:

Troops were decimated by illness.

Note that it is best not to use decimate – as many people do – to mean "to destroy completely." It is better to use a word like *destroy* or *annihilate* for this.

Different

The safest preposition to use with different is *from*, which is the same use as the related verb *differ from*:

> *These biscuits taste different from the other ones.*

In American English, but not British English, *than* can be used:

> *He has a different job than me.*

It is also considered acceptable in British, but not American English to use *to*:

> *Your circumstances are different to mine.*

Dilemma

The word dilemma comes from the Greek prefix *di-* meaning "two." Therefore, purists argue that it should only be used to describe a situation where there are two alternatives, and not where there are a wider range of alternatives:

> *To support my husband or my son: that was my dilemma.*

In formal writing, dilemma should not be used simply as a synonym of *problem*, but only for situations where some sort of choice or decision is to be made.

Because the original Greek word referred to two unpleasant alternatives, some people also believe that it should still only be used in this way, and not for a choice between two pleasant things.

Disinterested or uninterested?

In formal, modern English, uninterested is used to mean "not interested" and disinterested to mean "unbiased" or "impartial":

> *The audience seemed completely uninterested in what she had to say.*
> *We need a disinterested person to make a decision for us.*

However, in reality, the two words are used so interchangeably that even if you try to make the distinction, it is probably best to avoid *disinterested* altogether to avoid ambiguity, and use *unbiased* or *impartial* instead.

Double negatives

A double negative is the use of two negative words in the same sentence. These are common in some dialects of spoken English, but should never be used in writing.

> *I haven't got no money.* (Double negative.)
> *I haven't got any money.* (Standard English.)
> *She didn't tell me nothing.* (Double negative.)
> *She didn't tell me anything.* (Standard English.)

Equally

It is common to see sentences such as the following:

> *Their work was equally as good.*
> *His house is equally as large as Ava's.*

However, you should not use the word *as* with equally. Equally should come directly before the adjective:

> *Their work was equally good.*
> *His house and Ava's house are equally large.*

Farther/farthest or further/furthest?

If you use further/furthest all the time you can avoid any difficulty here. Some people, however, prefer to use farther when they are talking about literal distances:

> *We traveled farther into the mountains.*
> *Which car can go the farthest on a full tank of gas?*

Fewer or less?

Fewer should be used before plural nouns and less before uncountable nouns:

> *There are fewer pupils in her class than last year.*
> *I hope you'll have fewer problems this time.*
> *I'm trying to use less butter in my cooking.*
> *I had even less information about it than you.*

In formal writing, it is best to stick to this rule, but in more informal contexts it is common to see less used before plural nouns:

> *There were less people there than I expected.*
> *This checkout is for people with 10 items or less.*

It is acceptable even in formal English to use less before numbers:

> *I had seen him less than five times in my life.*

Hopefully

In current English it is common to see the word *hopefully* "it is hoped," usually at the beginning of a sentence, when what the speaker or writer really means is "I hope that":

> *Hopefully we won't have to wait long.*
> *Hopefully they'll pay us for the time we spent.*

However, some people object to this, saying that hopefully should only be used to mean "in a hopeful way":

> *He looked at her hopefully.*
> *We waited hopefully to see if she would appear.*

It is best to avoid overusing hopefully in formal writing as a sentence adverb because it provides an opportunity for others to criticize.

I or me?

You should avoid writing sentences such as *Tim and me cooked a meal.*

When you use two pronouns or a personal name and a pronoun together, think about whether they are the subject or the object of the sentence:

> *Tom and I went to the football match.* (Subject.)
> *He asked Jo and me to sweep all the floors.* (Object.)

If you are not sure whether to use I or me, imagine you were only writing about yourself and not the other person. For instance, you would say *I went to the football game*, so that is the form to use when you add the other person too.

Irregardless

This is not a word in standard English, so do not use it in your writing. The word you need is *regardless*.

Lend, loan and borrow

If you lend someone something, you let them use it for a while. If you borrow something, you take it from someone else to use for a while. In American English you can use *loan* as a verb, especially for amounts of money, in the same way you use *lend* for things. However, idioms always use lend; for example, *lend a hand* (=help) and *lend me your ears* (=listen)

> *Can you lend me a pen?*
> *Can you loan me 50 bucks till payday?*
> *Can I borrow your pen?*

Literally

This word should be used only to emphasize that what follows is exact fact, and is not being said in an exaggerated or figurative way:

> *The waves were literally as high as a house.*
> *She was literally penniless.*

It is common for literally to be used simply to emphasize what follows, but examples like this should be avoided in formal writing:

> *I literally jumped out of my skin.*
> *We literally had to wait for hours.*

Media

Strictly speaking, media is the plural form of the Latin *medium*. Some people insist that it should be used with a plural verb:

> *The media were guilty of invading her privacy.*

However, media is often used as a singular noun in current English:

> *The media is making the most of this scandal.*

If you want to talk about one particular form of communication though, you should use the singular *medium*:

> *She is of the view that television is a dangerous medium.*

Off (of)

The preposition *off* may or may not be followed by *of* in American English:

> *It fell off of the table.*
> *It fell off the table.*

Ought

Unlike with the other modal verbs (*can, might, must*, etc.), *ought*, is normally followed by a *to* infinitive. Some speakers, however, leave off the *to* when *ought* is used with a negative:

> *You ought to visit Margie while you're here.*
> *Oughtn't we see if he's all right?*
> *You ought not to leave your keys in the door.*

Out

The word *out* is usually an adverb:

> *I dropped my bag and all my money fell out.*
> *I'm not going to go out today.*

You can use *out* as a preposition, but it is considered informal without *of* after it:

> *She threw the bag out the window.* (Informal.)
> *I walked out of the room.*

Per

The most common use of this preposition is to show a mathematical relationship between quantities or numbers:

> *They were paid $100 per performance.*
> *The speed limit here is 40 miles per hour.*

In business jargon it is used as a shorthand substitute for "with reference to" or "concerning," but you should avoid this use in formal writing:

> *Per your request yesterday I have sent out three cases.*
> (Business jargon.)

Phenomena

Remember that phenomena is the plural of phenomenon. Do not use phenomena as a singular:

> *Lightning is a natural phenomena.* (Incorrect.)
> *Lightning is a natural phenomenon.* (Correct.)

Plus

Plus is mainly a preposition whose meaning is similar to the conjunction *and* (as in "three plus two equals five"). *Plus* can also be used as a conjunction with a meaning similar to *and*. When it joins clauses rather than phrases, however, some people object to its use and so you should avoid it in formal writing:

> *He came in late, plus he didn't have a ticket.* (Informal.)

The reason being

Do not use the verb *is* after this phrase, because it does not relate grammatically. You should use *that*:

> *We had to sell the business, the reason being that my husband was ill.*

Refute

This word is often used simply to mean "deny," but this is not correct, standard use. Refute means to prove something wrong with evidence.

> *With these documents, he was able to refute the allegations.*

So

So is one of the commonest adverbs in English and most of its uses are not controversial. It has recently developed a new use as an intensifying or emphatic adverb that modifies the predicate of a sentence and many people disapprove of this usage, so it is best to avoid it in all except informal writing.

> *She so doesn't need to have another kid.* (Informal.)
> *That is so what I wanted you to tell me.* (Informal.)

Split infinitives

A split infinitive happens when you write an adverb between *to* and a verb, e.g., *to finally agree*.

A lot of people do not like this, although plenty of great writers such as Donne, Eliot and Browning have used it.

> *We were asked to carefully look inside the box.* (Split infinitive.)
> *We were asked to look carefully inside the box.*

In a few cases, a split infinitive is necessary to avoid a change in meaning:

> *He failed to completely understand my point.* (Split infinitive, but means that he did not understand everything about the point.)
> *He completely failed to understand my point.* (This has a different meaning – that he was unable to understand the point at all.)
> *He failed to understand my point completely.* (This could have either meaning, and is therefore ambiguous.)

Sure and surely

Both these words can be used as adverbs but their meaning and register is not the same. In general, *sure* is more informal and is used when the speaker or writer expects agreement:

> *The children sure like the new jungle gym in the playground.*
> *You sure are late!*

Surely is more likely to be used in formal contexts, and where the writer or speaker is trying to persuade:

> *I surely didn't mean to cause any offense.*
> *Surely you don't think that he'll actually answer the letter.*

Try

It is acceptable to use *and* or *to* after try, though *and* is slightly less formal:

> *Try and find the coin.*
> *We will try to help you.*

Used to

Note that when using the negative and question forms with used to, you need to drop the *d* from *used*. This is because the tense marker is now carried by whatever form of the verb *do* is used:

> *Years ago, children used to be more polite.*
> *I used to hate broccoli, but now I like it.*
> *Children didn't use to have TVs in their bedrooms.*
> *Did you use to play football when you were a child?*

In a very formal style, we could write:

> *I used not to have a car.*

Way

Way as an adverb is often used before a preposition or another adverb for emphasis, and is somewhat more informal than *far* would be in the same context:

> *You're driving way over the speed limit.*
> *There is way too much sugar in these children's diet.*

Some people use *way* as an intensifying adverb before an adjective. This use is regarded as slang by many people and should be avoided in all except informal writing:

> *That was a way stupid thing to do.* (Informal.)
> *Her Mom's really strict but her Dad is way cool.* (Informal.)

Who or whom?

Who is now commonly used as the object where in the past it was only considered correct to use whom:

> *Who do you work for?*

If you use whom in sentences like this, your writing will sound extremely formal:

> *For whom do you work?*

However, you must use whom directly after a preposition:

> *The woman to whom I spoke was a local nurse.*
> *There were twenty masked prisoners, many of whom were armed.*

Index

A

abbreviations 114, 120, 251
Abbreviations 88
abstract 166
Abstract 158
Abstract nouns 211
Acronyms 90
active verbs 48, 49
Adjectives 217
adverbials 245
Adverbs 221
Agreement 98, 233
Alliteration 71
Alternative plurals 273
ambiguity 53
animate noun 211
Antonym 71
apostrophe 238
Apostrophes 98
Appendices 168
Assonance 71
attitude 57
Auxiliary verbs 208
Avoiding clichés 50
Avoiding offense 64

B

Bar charts 31
bare infinitive 207
bibliography 85
Bibliography 159, 168
blog 140
bloggers 140
bold 22
boxes 28
Brackets 259
bullets 165, 194
Bullets 23

C

Capital letters 87, 98, 249
CAPITAL LETTERS 22
Cardinal numbers 224
CD-ROM 69
change of style 62
charts 165
Charts 29
clip art 27
Collective nouns 211
comma 243
commas 47
Common mistakes 295
Common nouns 211
comparative 217, 223
Compound nouns 211
Compound tenses 227
computer 100
Concluding 186
Conclusion 156, 159
Conclusions 37, 175
Concrete nouns 211
congratulating 137
Conjunctions 226
contact details 203
Contents list 166
context 67
Contracted forms 241
contractions 114
Contractions 241, 277
controversial issues 295
copyright 27
Countable nouns 212
cover letter 131
Cross-references 99
crossword puzzles 67
CV 187

D

Dangling participles 298

Dashes 262
dates 246
Dates 93, 99
definite article 224
Demonstrative pronouns 214
demonstratives 224
Determiners 224
diagrams 29, 165, 196
dictionary 69
direct speech 76
Direct speech 247
Disability 66
discourse markers 246
dissertation 157
distributives 224
Double negatives 301
draft 15

E

ellipsis 83
Email 104
em dash 262
emoticon 119
emoticons 115
Emphasis 60
en dash 262
Essays 144
Etymology 70
Euphemism 71
Example sentences 70
exclamation point 254
exclamatives 224
Executive summary 166

F

figurative 53
Figurative language 72
flow chart 8
flyers 198
Fonts 22

footers 26
footnote 85
Foreign words and
  phrases 94
formal 55
formality 48
Formal or work letters
  123
Future continuous 230
Future perfect 228
Future perfect
  continuous 230
Future simple 228

G

Geographical terms 86
glossary 168
grammar 98
Graphs 30

H

Headers 26
headings 165
Headings 39, 62
Homophones 97, 280
hyphen 260
hyphens 21

I

Idioms 72
images 27
imperative form 191
improve your spelling
  267
inanimate noun 211
Increasing your
  vocabulary 67
indefinite article 224
Indefinite pronouns 214
indirect object 232
indirect speech 76

infinitive 207
informal 55
initialism 90
instant messaging 106
Instructions 191
Internet dictionaries 69
Interrogative pronouns
  214
Intransitive verbs 206
introduction 182
Introduction 167
Introductions 35, 170
Irregular inflections 70
Irregular plurals 272
irregular verbs 231
italics 22

J

jargon 48

L

Latin 295
Latin words 56, 89
layout 18, 123
Leaflets 198
letterhead 124
letter of inquiry 133
links 141
list 23, 194
literal 53
literary 56

M

Main verbs 206
Making notes 11
Marking your
  corrections 101
Mass nouns 212
meaning 53
Metaphor 72
mind maps 7

Modal verbs 209
Ms 124

N

names 245, 251
Names of people 86
notes 179
Nouns 211
Numbered lists 25
Numbers 91, 99

O

object 232
ordering 34
ordinal numbers 224
Outlines 13

P

page numbers 26
paper 157
paragraphs 20, 146, 165
Paragraphs 42
paraphrasing 84
Paraphrasing 185
Parentheses 258
passive form 194
Past continuous 229
Past perfect 228
Past perfect continuous
  230
Past simple 227
period 251
Personal pronouns 213
Pictograms 32
pictures 196
Pie charts 30
plagiarize 144
plagiarizing 12, 81
plain English 48
planning 145
Planning 2

plurals 271
poetic language 56
possession 238
Possessive pronouns 213
possessives 224
prefixes 268
Prepositions 225
Presentations 176
Present continuous 229
Present perfect 228
Present perfect
  continuous 230
Present simple 227
primary auxiliaries 208
print preview 18
prompt cards 179
pronouns 53
Pronouns 213
Pronunciation 70
pronunciations 69
proofreading 101
Proper nouns 86, 211
Proverbs 73
punctuation 98
Punctuation 62, 114, 120

Q
quantifiers 224
question mark 80, 253
Questions 79
question tags 80
quotation marks 76
Quotation marks 247
quotations 12, 155, 174
Quotations 81

R
Race 64
Recommendations 168
redundancy 52
References 99
Referencing quotations
  84

Reflexive pronouns 213
Regional information 70
Register 55, 70
Regular 231
Relative pronouns 214
religion 64
Repetition 61, 99
reported speech 76, 246
Reported speech 77
Reports 162
Research 9
résumé 187

S
Salutations 105, 119
sans-serif 22
semicolon 257
Sentence adverbs 222
sentence tags 245
Sentence tags 80
serif 22
sexism 65
signoff 115, 121
Silent letters 276
simile 51
Similes 73
Simple tenses 227
slash 264
slides 180, 183
small caps 22
smiley 119
smileys 115
Speech 76
spellchecker 147
spelling 97, 266
spider maps 7
style 44
Subject 232
Subject lines 106
Suffixes 268
summaries 11
Summarizing 185
summary 3

superlative 217, 223
supporting auxiliary
  208
Syllabification 70
syllables 267
Synonyms 73

T
tab key 25
Table of contents 158
tables 165
Tables 28
tautology 52
technical terms 56, 203
Tenses 227
the Internet 10
the passive 113
thesaurus 68
thesis 157
title 195
Title Page 158, 166
titles 87, 201
tone 131
Tone 57, 111, 119
trademark 87
Transitive verbs 206
Typeface 61
typefaces 22
typo 147

U
Uncountable nouns 212
underlining 22
UPPER-CASE LETTERS
  113

V
Variant spellings 70
Venn diagrams 31
verb phrase 206
verbs 210
visual aids 183
vocabulary notebook 67